# Christ and Counter- Christ

*Apocalyptic Themes in Theology and Culture*

## Carl E. Braaten

FORTRESS PRESS
PHILADELPHIA

*To My*

*Children*

Craig, Martha, Maria,

and Kristofer

Copyright © 1972 by Fortress Press

All rights reserved. No part of this publication may be reproduced, stored in a retrieval system or transmitted in any form or by any means, electronic, mechanical, photocopying, recording or otherwise, without prior permission of the copyright owner.

*Library of Congress Catalog Card Number 76-171493*

*ISBN 0-8006-0120-3*

2965F71     Printed in USA     1-120

# Contents

## PART TWO
## COUNTER-CULTURAL CONCRETIONS

# Introduction:
# The Renaissance of
# Apocalyptic

I had completed this manuscript before I discovered a small but significant book on apocalypticism written by Klaus Koch, entitled *Ratlos vor der Apokalyptik* (Gütersloher Verlagshaus Gerd Mohn, 1970). He subtitles his book a "Streitschrift"—a fighting document. My book is also a polemic. Apocalyptic material has a way of heating the ovens of theological thought; its chief symbols magnify distances and differences; its style of thought is two-dimensional; it accelerates the dialectics of negativity and transcendence. A prior reading of Koch's book would have sharpened my insights into the apocalyptic thought-world; it could have helped me to interpret its relevance to current problems of theology and the present cultural situation. I am grateful that at least in this "introduction"—to be read as a "postscript"—I can acknowledge Koch's work on apocalyptic as a confirmation of the direction in which my theology is moving.

The conviction is growing within me that apocalypticism holds the key to a number of problems in theology. The first is the problem of Christian origins, so important to the question of Christian identity that is being raised by every church today and by each sensitive believer. To those who are fed up with biblical theology and find the auxiliary disciplines of theology more challenging—e.g., philosophy, psychology, and sociology—we can say that the rediscovery of the relevance of apocalyptic is opening up new frontiers of biblical research. It is true that biblical theology in the age of neo-orthodoxy fell into a kind of scholasticism, which made the transition from biblical categories to modern dogmatics appear smooth and obvious. Exegetes were dogmaticians and dogmaticians were exegetes, showing scant awareness of the hermeneutical problem. The Bible seemed to support everyone's favorite brand of orthodoxy. Now, with the resurgence of apocalyptic, the underpinnings of orthodoxy become more shaky, because apocalyptic enjoys only a marginal status within the biblical canon.

Second, the phenomenon of apocalyptic can provide a better historical binding between the Old and the New Testaments. Biblical theology makes no sense if it remains exclusively within the limits of the traditional canon, for the reason that the Old Testament does not report the full religio-historical situation out of which the New Testament arose. The New Testament is a literary occurrence largely within the medium of apocalyptic. This is the gist of what Albert Schweitzer was saying; it is the meaning of Ernst Käsemann's dictum: "Apocalyptic was after all the mother of all Christian theology." We may be standing on the threshold of a truly historical reconstruction of Christian origins.

Third, the new appreciation of apocalyptic can help us to construct a more adequate picture of the historical Jesus. The tendency to ethicize the Jesus of history remains strong, permitting an easy transference of the ethics of Jesus to the modern situation. In spite of Albert Schweitzer's achievement, ethics is too often the core of the Christology in the recent existentialist, linguistical, and secularization approaches to theology. The urge to portray an unapocalyptic Jesus is linked to an unexamined assumption that apocalypticism carries too many liabilities to be useful in contemporary theology. This assumption has been overturned by the work of Wolfhart Pannenberg. The full eschatological conception of the kingdom of God is the key to a Christology grounded in the historical Jesus and capable of meaningful interpretation today.

Fourth, picking up the thread of apocalyptic can shed new light on the history of Christianity. It can help us to spotlight the new that Christianity brought into the history of mankind, in terms of historical consciousness, the futurist hope, the sources of revolution and the utopian imagination that has nourished modern forms of democracy and socialism. The apocalyptic perspective depicts Christianity as a movement of history in quest of the kingdom of God, rather than as the established religion in the Constantinian order.

Fifth, apocalyptic sources broaden the theological outlook beyond mere personalism. Theology has tended to give the lion's share of attention to the personal and the private, the inner-worldly and the otherworldly, the sensitive conscience, the decisional experience and the salvation of the individual soul. Apocalyptic theology, with all its stress on the power of the negative, never fails to drive toward the universal horizon. It seeks the most comprehensive viewpoint, and therefore has an eye to dimensions of power and righteousness in the cross-currents of the world.

Sixth, the apocalyptic outlook invites us to look into a society from the bottom up rather than from the top down. Christian institutions are still living under their Constantinian license, deriving their social legitimacy from the top. It is still largely true that Christianity functions in society as a religion, that is, as opium of the masses, and as the ideological tool of the ruling classes. Perhaps nothing could be more useful than a renaissance of the apocalyptic vision born in the graveyards, the catacombs, at the bottom of society or outside the gate.

Seventh, the symbols of the apocalypse can challenge Western Christianity to transcend itself. The majority of Christians in America think of the church as part of the "establishment." When young people are "turned off" by what they experience in the West, they don't look to the church for an alternative, but they turn to the East. The church, however, is called to mediate transcendence—distance from the present—in every situation. The orientation to Eastern mysticism is an eloquent sign that the church has become so much a part of the situation that it has lost its power to generate criticism, to occasion ecstasy, and to open the future. I believe that the better way is to probe our own historical origins, to achieve identity through continuity with our past, to strike the arteries of fresh promise and new possibilities embedded in the events which the Scriptures report.

Finally, the intention of this book, despite its partially polemic form, is apologetic. The purpose is to show that in the present critical situation our hope for the future becomes recognizable in the event on which Christianity is based—the Christ-event. The one who says, "I believe in Jesus Christ," means to confess that in him the eschatological future of the world and of the whole of humanity has dawned.

# Part One

# Theological
# Foundations

# 1

# Apocalyptic

# Interpretation of

# History

## THE ONGOING DEBATE ON APOCALYPTICISM

One of the liveliest debates in current biblical scholarship is the role and significance of apocalypticism in late Jewish and early Christian theology.[1] Even while the outcome of the debate remains in some doubt, I believe that it is possible and useful to appropriate some of the fundamental categories of biblical apocalyptic in constructing a systematic theology of history. We know very well from past history that systematic theologians cannot wait for biblical scholars to reach a consensus before interpreting the data that result from historical research. In the midst of diverging historical judgments, the theologian has to risk a decision if facts of history form a part of the contents of faith he is committed to interpret. We also know well enough that very often a particular historian reports his findings in a way that reflects his own religious bias; therefore, systematic theologians have no reason to be overly timid in face of the historical problem. In fact, there can be a fruitful two-way traffic between historical research and theological imagination, so that an insight into the contemporary religious relevance of apocalyptic categories may free the historical scholar to acknowledge more cheerfully what the facts suggest. I am convinced, for example, that New Testament historians have been reluctant to accept the full weight of Albert Schweitzer's discovery of the apocalyptic structure of Jesus' eschatology because they agreed with his conclusion that the Jewishness of Jesus' apocalypticism makes him a stranger to modern culture. Even while they could concede some truth to Schweitzer's thesis, they were busy searching for some *unapocalyptic* essence in Jesus' ministry that could be salvaged for modern appropriation. The existentialist interpretation of Jesus' kerygma is one example of the attempt to mine something out of the historical Jesus while dismissing the apocalyptic elements as so much mythological husk that can be blown away. Surely today there can hardly be a scholar who fails to see that the cradling of Jesus in the categories of "kerygma" and "existence" is less the result of Gospel research than a hermeneutical adjustment to the philosophy of Heidegger.[2]

The uniformity of the Bultmann school was first strained when Gerhard Ebeling and Ernst Fuchs renewed the quest of the historical Jesus in order to secure some material continuity between the pre-Easter kerygma *of* Jesus and the post-Easter kerygma *about* Jesus.[3] They agreed that it was the *faith* of Jesus that uniquely gave rise to the kerygma, his own and the early church's. It is well known that Bultmann declined the amendment of his pupils,[4] preferring instead to hold to his original position of discontinuity between the historical Jesus and the christological kerygma after Easter. However, this was all a skirmish that could be contained within the school. The basic terms of discussion remained in force, even when differences were being spelled out. It was Ernst Käsemann who first began to widen the terms of the discussion by reopening the question of apocalypticism that Bultmann had so successfully silenced by his demythologizing. Käsemann aroused his colleagues from their hermeneutic slumbers by this provocative announcement: "Apocalyptic was the mother of all Christian theology."[5] When future historians of theology look back upon our period, I think they might say this statement signaled the demise of Bultmannian theology. Bultmannian theology will rank second only to Tillich's as the most creative apologetic for Christian faith in the first half of the twentieth century. However, its most glaring failure as an apologetic was twofold: its reckless handling of biblical apocalyptic and its blindness to the relevance of apocalyptic in the interpretation of history.[6] Our most illuminating philosophical, political, and theological categories in the interpretation of history have their roots in biblical apocalypticism.[7] Since Bultmann did not find it theologically relevant to interpret history, but only existence, he could neutralize these categories without feeling any loss to Christian theology.

The response of Ebeling and Fuchs to Käsemann's rehabilitation of apocalyptic and the debate that ensued can give us a modest beginning for a more far-reaching theological appropriation of the apocalyptic consciousness and its insights into the dialectics of the divine and the demonic, or of Christ and Counter-Christ, in history and the cosmos. Käsemann is a New Testament theologian who makes it none of his business to escort his findings to a pleasing systematic conclusion. In a caustic remark directed at Ebeling and Fuchs, who had complained that Käsemann seemed to take no responsibility for the theological consequences of his historical investigations, Käsemann says that "in the present flood tide of 'interpretation' there must be some who devote themselves to administering the legacy of the historians, if only to disturb the interpreters."[8] Käsemann realized that he was taking up one of the forbidden topics in theology and the established church. Pointing at theology, he wrote, "Primitive Christian apocalyptic is generally regarded by theological scholars as not being a suitable topic for our day."[9] Pointing at the church, he rightly observed that apocalyptic has "seldom enjoyed the goodwill of the dominant church and its theology."[10] There is no denying that the theology of the church has largely seen its task in the overcoming of apocalyptic."[11] The apocalyptic hope in history has driven the church to abandon established positions, to make it an exodus-movement in quest of the kingdom of God.[12] Such a movement inevitably transgressed the limits of official orthodoxy, entering upon novelties that at the time looked like heresies.

Ebeling calls attention to this connection between apocalyptic and heresy: "According to the prevailing ecclesiastical and theological tradition, supremely also of the Reformation, apocalyptic . . . is to say the least a suspicious symptom of tendencies towards heresy."[13]

Käsemann is aware that the renewal of apocalyptic will undermine the official theology of the church, which became what it is by getting rid of its mother—apocalypticism—and accepting Hellenism as its godfather.[14] If apocalyptic is essential to primitive Christianity, then its recovery will make the relations between orthodoxy and heresy much more fluid. However, the implicit butt of Käsemann's attack is not orthodoxy as such; rather, it is the tendency of recent existentialist theology to dehistoricize the kerygma, to break the continuity of history into existential moments, to dissolve the history of salvation into the historicity of existence, and to reduce the future of God to the futurity of man. This way an existential ethic replaces a historical eschatology; the kerygma becomes mere address, not narrative history. The Bultmannians put anthropology at the beginning of primitive Christian theology; Käsemann sees apocalyptically determined historical thinking as the original form. It's not the case that primitive Christian theology was later apocalypticized, although that also happened to excess; rather, apocalyptic was there from the start, and most assuredly also throughout Paul's writings.

But there is a problem with Käsemann's handling of apocalyptic; he traces it back to Easter but not to the historical Jesus. The message of John the Baptist was apocalyptically determined, but not so with Jesus. "His own preaching was not constitutively stamped by apocalyptic."[15] Instead, Jesus preached the immediate nearness of God; in preaching the near *basileia* he becomes the form in which the eschatological age becomes present. Lacking in Jesus' preaching are characteristic marks of apocalyptic, such as awaiting the coming of the Son of Man, the restoration of the Twelve Tribes in the messianic kingdom, and the imminent dawning of the parousia. It was only due to the impact of Easter and Pentecost

that the post-Easter church resorted to apocalyptic concepts
to interpret the personal achievement of Jesus. But this only
poses again the problem of continuity between Jesus and the
Easter kerygma in a new way. Käsemann cannot explain historically how to ground the apocalyptic message of the early
church in the unapocalyptic fact of Jesus. It seems as though
Käsemann is still sticking to the traditional argument of a
fundamental distinction between "eschatology" and "apocalyptic." Hence, one can presumably imagine a pure eschatology in Jesus, without the contamination of apocalyptic
fantasies. On this point the debate on apocalypticism is
carried further by another group of scholars quite outside
the Bultmannian fold. They go all the way to include Jesus
within the context of apocalyptic, and draw the person and
preaching of Jesus directly into the beginnings of Christian
theology. This is the point of view that linked together all the
scholars that were more or less closely associated with Wolfhart Pannenberg, and who are often, but now misleadingly,
referred to as the "Pannenberg group."

Ulrich Wilkens, the New Testament theologian of this
"group,"[16] acknowledges that Jesus is not an apocalyptist and
does not indulge his imagination in pure speculations about a
remote future, as so many of the apocalyptists did. Yet there
is no way to grasp the self-understanding of Jesus and the
meaning of his activity except against the historical background of apocalyptic expectations. He cannot be accounted
for within the framework of Pharisaic and rabbinic theology.
Jesus' attack against the Torah could not possibly arise from
within the rabbinic tradition. Instead, his unique self-
consciousness matured into an awareness of his own authority, so that he could place himself against the authority of the
law. This unique personal authority which Jesus claimed
could most understandably emerge within a consciousness
that was oriented to a compelling new reality far superior to
all the prestigious traditions of the past. Apocalyptic theology
provided just such conditions within which a present prolep-
sis of the eschatological future could assert its superiority

over the law,[17] even while acknowledging God as its giver. The law is not a once-for-all gift, but a contingent event of history directed by a personally free God. Although Jesus was not an apocalyptist,[18] his proclamation grew out of the conceptual tradition found in Jewish apocalyptic faith. The central *basileia* concept in Jesus' preaching bears the indelible stamp of its apocalyptic origin.

Equally significant in the current debate is how apocalyptic was modified by Jesus' preaching.[19] The fact that many scholars are reluctant to link the eschatology of Jesus with late Jewish apocalyptic may be explained by the fact that Jesus brought about a massive concentration of apocalyptic expectation in his own activity. The apocalyptic outlook on the future is intentionally curved back on the present activity of Jesus. He does not merely point to the future in the present; instead, he makes present the realities of the future in a concentrated way. The attitude that a person takes to Jesus now determines his own personal destiny. This is the material point of continuity between the historical Jesus and the post-Easter kerygma. The disciple's relation to Jesus is his point of entry to the salvation coming with the new age. So even before Easter there was an embryonic Christology bound up with apocalyptic. Therefore, Käsemann's statement that apocalyptic was the mother of all Christian theology can encompass also the foundational role of the historical Jesus in the Christian faith.

## THE DUALIZATION OF THE WORLD AS HISTORY

We have been using the term "apocalyptic" in the conspicuously imprecise way in which it appears in the literature on the subject.[20] Ebeling rightly charged that Käsemann never defined what he meant by the term. Käsemann replied that he always uses it to describe the near expectation of the parousia. August Strobel sees the essence of apocalyptic in the idea of a transcendent supranatural inbreaking of the kingdom. Wilkens sees it, rather, as an interpretation of history from the perspective of its end point. Cullmann uses the term in its etymological sense to denote a special class of literature in which there is recorded a "revelation of final secrets."[21] Also in widespread use is the derogatory sense of the term as dreamlike speculations that have nothing to do with the historical present. Gerhard von Rad has contributed to this depreciation of apocalyptic, and has thus triggered off another aspect of the debate. In his judgment, the origins of apocalyptic do not lie in the prophetic view of history at all, but in wisdom. Thus he can say it is "really devoid of all theology. This view of history lacks all confessional character. . . . Indeed, we may even ask whether apocalyptic literature had any existential relationship with history at all."[22] Confusing the issue still more, Hans Dieter Betz places both Jewish and Christian apocalyptic within the larger context of Hellenistic syncretism and gnosticism. It is not a "purely inner-Jewish phenomenon"[23] with special roots in the early traditions of Israel's religion. So we are faced with many open questions on which we can only hope for further light from scholarly analysis of the Qumran material.

I am going to suggest, however, that we may have the key to the essence of apocalypticism in one of its most depreciated features. That is its dualism, the juxtaposition of the two aeonic powers.[24] Dualism, like apocalypticism itself, has suffered from a bad theological reputation. In his book, *The Relevance of Apocalyptic,* H. H. Rowley can only say, "We are much too philosophical to tolerate such an idea."[25] I think theology will have to overcome such dainty philosophical elegance that would cause it to shrink from the two-dimensional thinking of biblical apocalyptic. History is not a straight line of progress moving forward on one track. Rather, the course of history moves forward through the mediation of mutually antagonistic forces. In biblical apocalyptic the world becomes historical through the process of dualization. This is not just one characteristic alongside many others, such as esotericism, gnosticism, pseudonymity, numerology, mysticism, magic, etc.[26] The heart of apocalyptic is its historico-eschatological dualism, the dialectical differentiation of all reality into this present evil age and the blessed one to come. As II Esdras puts it: "God has made not one world but two." The new world that is coming is mediated through a negation of the old, that is, *ex oppositione*. In more abstract terms, negativity is the midwife of creativity; in symbolic terms, the cross is the apocalypse of death as the way of salvation, and the resurrection is a means of expressing symbolically this negation of life with which the eschatological future identifies itself.

Karl Rahner, in an essay that predates the current rehabilitation of apocalyptic theology, entitled "The Hermeneutics of Eschatological Assertions," offered the following definitions: "To extrapolate from the present into the future is eschatology, to interpolate from the future into the present is apocalyptic."[27] At that time he was of the opinion that Christianity can go with eschatology, but that apocalyptic is a degeneration. Rahner's distinction is useful in that it exposes a fundamental difference between two approaches to the future. The expression "theology of hope" is commonly used carelessly to cover two quite different systems of thought. The one could be described as an evolutionary monism (Teilhard de Chardin); the other could be called a revolutionary dualism. The former thinks of eschatology as the extrapolation from the present to the future; its key concept is *development*. The latter thinks of eschatology as the power of the future entering the present through creative negation; its key concept is *liberation*.

The difference between *development* and *liberation* may become more clear if we switch from philosophical abstractions to political concretions.[28] Development means growth. Human beings and human communities need to grow; we speak of them as underdeveloped. Developed nations want to assist the underdeveloped nations in achieving their stature. The ideology of development is the philosophy of liberalism extending itself into foreign policy. The advanced nations, especially the capitalist economies, are all in favor of devel-

opment. The facts, however, indicate that the idea of
development does not grasp the real state of affairs. The
international agencies that control the world economy believe
in development. Understandably, those who already enjoy
power and wealth would welcome a self-aggrandizing extrapolation of their present into the future. But they have
reason to tremble before the idea of liberation that proclaims
a revolutionary negation of the causes of oppression. Those
who see themselves as exiles, aliens, oppressed, enslaved do
not think in terms of development. That does not touch the
tragic dimensions of their plight. And they know that liberation will only come through a negation of those powers,
structures, and trends that seek to dominate through a further
development of their present systems of control. Well, that is
just a political illustration of the possible difference between
two types of approach to the future.

I believe that our knowledge of Jesus' preaching of the
kingdom of God puts us in the position to reverse Karl
Rahner's judgment on apocalyptic. That it may not appear
we are making things too easy for ourselves, we will appeal to
Bultmann's treatment of the historical Jesus, and not Käsemann's or Pannenberg's. So clearly he states: "Future and
present are not related in the sense that the Kingdom begins
as a historical fact in the present and achieves its fulfillment
in the future."[29] Further, he states, the idea of development
is a Hellenistic intrusion, and this comes out most conspicuously when the future kingdom is thought of as the consum-
mation of creation, as though there were an ascending line
from the beginning to the end. "In that case the Kingdom
would be already present in germ in the creation, and the
Kingdom would be the unfolding of these potentialities.
Then ideally the Kingdom would already exist in the present,
and its purely future character would be destroyed. But there
can be no doubt that according to Jesus' thought the Kingdom is the marvelous, new, wholly other, the opposite of
everything present."[30] In Jesus' preaching, God is the power
of the future contradicting all history that wishes to build its

future out of its present. That is history turned in upon itself; its vision of the future is only a far-off version of the present.

There are two Latin words for future: *futurum* and *adventus*.[31] *Futurum*, the future participle of *fuo*, the same root from which we get our word physics (*physis* in Greek comes from *phyo*) is the future actualization of potentialities within things. *Adventus* is the appearance of something new that is not yet within things, not even as potentiality. *Futurum* allows for the becoming of the present, its extrapolation; *adventus* announces the coming of the future, the interpolation of new reality. Christian eschatology is not metaphysical finalism but apocalyptic adventism, if the Christian doctrine of the future is to be developed in line with the thought forms of the New Testament.

Apocalyptic future brings new reality through creative negation. That is the heart of the apocalyptic process of history. Man entered upon a new career when he began to think of reality as history that can be split in two. He acquired the capacity to rise above his natural environment, which he shared with the other animals, by temporalizing his being and all being, and by splitting being and time into the here and now—the present—and the there and then—the future. Almost all of his cultural activities, his magic. mysticism, religion, philosophy, art, and technology have been created to help him cope with his dichotomized world, since he knows he stands between this world and another world, whether ideal, heavenly, supernatural, wholly future, or whatever. He is a man with dual citizenship. Again in our culture this truth is coming home to us, when after a strong dose of what Herbert Marcuse calls the one-dimensionalism[32] of our philosophy, politics, science, and technology, many people are calling off the world, and looking toward joining another world, full of bliss and beauty.

There is a revival of apocalyptic negation in our culture, but mostly in terms of its historic distortions, for example, the zealotism of the Weathermen and the asceticism of the Qumran-like Hippies who drop out of society. Jesus came

preaching the kingdom of God, releasing into life a greater
power than his contemporary Zealots to bring radical change,
and unlike the Essenes he practiced his freedom in the company of worldly people.[33] Jesus modified apocalypticism,
because he himself claimed to be the personal place where
the future of hope could happen now. There was nothing like
this in traditional apocalypticism. But he did not tone down
its negations. Jesus spoke in antitheses; his mind was marked
by the dualistic oppositions of apocalyptic thought; his
clearest clues to the future could be expressed in unrelenting
contradiction of established beliefs and practices. He was
animated by the power of negative thinking. He did not
imagine that the kingdom could come or that a person could
enter the kingdom except through a negation of existing
reality. He brought his power of negation to the side of those
who were left out, those who were being negated. In this way
he showed his negation was not destructive rejection, but
creative affirmation of sinners in search of freedom and
righteousness. The power of negation in Jesus was not a
movement toward nothingness. The dynamite he brought
was charged with hope that could blast away at the rigid
systems, institutions, and doctrines that kept men enslaved.
It was an invitation to join the exodus from the old and
dying age—the *ancien régime*—to the new world of the
kingdom of God.

The dynamism of the future is joined to a dialectic of
opposites. The path of history runs through this dialectic of
contradiction, and there is no immanent resolution in history,
and not *in* future history either, but only through a transcendent eschatological future *of* history. The *coincidentia
oppositorum* is not attainable through a process of formal
transcending in pure concepts, as in the line from Cusanus
to Hegel.[34] The Marxist criticism of idealism is valid; the
negative principle must sink its teeth into the material of
history and not rescind the oppositions in a heaven of abstract
thought.[35] So the transcendent reconciliation of antagonisms

can occur only eschatologically, for when all negativities are removed, history will have reached its final goal.

Classical negative theology is usually traced back to the influence of Greek philosophy on Christian thought. To the extent that this is true, it lost its footing in history. But it can again assert its rights if it rediscovers its apocalyptic ground, thus keeping the power of the negative principle at work within the dialectical logic of history. I don't think it is a pure coincidence that simultaneous with the recovery of biblical apocalytic there is occurring a new affirmation of Hegel in philosophical theology. For we could say that apocalyptic is the grandmother of Hegel's dialectical logic.[36] This is not a far-fetched statement, in light of the fact that the first attempts of the young Hegel to work out a system of categories occurred through a process of studying the text of the Gospels. That Hegel himself could disregard the need for an eschatological resolution of conflicts in history is due to the fact that he was satisfied with a reconciliation at the level of abstract thought. At least his radical disciples were fortunately not so easily convinced, since their experience in history indicated that man is still alienated from his essential destiny. But they in turn have become content with a purely secular eschatology, without transcendence. Christianity without eschatology and Marxism without transcendence are two heresies fighting each other. We are saying that "to get it all together" theology will have to retrace its steps to at least these two important crossroads: first, when early Christian apocalyptic became Hellenized, and second, when Hegel's empire was divided between his two unruly sons, Søren Kierkegaard and Karl Marx.

The negative principle in apocalyptic may provide insight toward a new formulation of the doctrine of God. The supernatural God of Hellenistic orthodoxy does not easily lay hold of history; he prefers to remain in heaven. The apocalyptic God approaches history with oppositional power, in order that through crisis and conflict the existing reality may give way to a counter-reality. God is not *super*natural, but *contra*natural, neither this-worldly, i.e., purely immanent, nor otherworldly, i.e., purely transcendent, but a new reality, hitherto unknown, approaching history to negate the powers that rule within it, in order to establish a kingdom not of this world. Perhaps Pannenberg's phrase "God does not yet exist"[37] is not wholly felicitous, but it is well chosen to express the qualitative difference between all existing reality and the eschatological otherness of a God who makes himself manifest first of all as the power of contradiction, of criticism, in crisis, on the cross, and not in smooth continuity as the consummator and converging center of a continuing creation. Theology still must decide whether Aristotle or Jesus is the teacher of God and how he relates or disrelates to the world. That sounds very Tertullian, but then again the apocalyptic tradition retained more of its original vitality in him than in some of his orthodox opponents.

## CHRIST AND COUNTER-CHRIST TODAY

The essence of the negative principle and its dualizing function comes most clearly to expression in relation to the symbol of the Counter-Christ in primitive Christian apocalyptic. Whenever Christianity has lacked the imagination to identify the Counter-Christ[38] at work in history, its preaching of the gospel has been reduced to law. There is no doubt that the church itself has felt that the apocalyptic symbol of Counter-Christ is a scandalous part of its own eschatological gospel. For either the Counter-Christ appears as a tyrant on the throne of an empire, in which the church wants to be the favored religion, or the Counter-Christ appears as the Grand Inquisitor[39] at the top of the church's hierarchy, persecuting the faithful while claiming to be the successor of Christ. Since the very beginning of Christian apocalyptic the tradition has wavered between the concept of the Counter-Christ as a demonic power incarnate in a political figure like Nero and as a false messiah rising up in the midst of the people of God themselves. The early Christians favored the political interpretation, seeing the emperor as the incarnation of the Dragon, but when Christianity became established and the emperor was officially a Christian, the Counter-Christ was looked for within the church.[40] From Joachim di Fiore to Martin Luther the ecclesiastical interpretation became popular; the Counter-Christ took over the Roman papacy at the height of its power under Gregory VII. The migration of the Counter-Christ from the state to the church was not an arbitrary whim of popular consciousness. Rather, a definite criterion was implicitly operative; the issue was slavery and freedom. Luther made it clear that not the person of the pope but the power of the papacy was opposed to Christ, because it attached enslaving conditions to the gospel that makes man free.[41]

The important thing in Luther's interpretation is not his material judgment that the papacy is the locus of the Counter-Christ. That no longer has any validity simply because the papacy is not a giant among the powers of the modern world. History has stripped the papacy of most of its power, so that it no longer functions as the cruel oppressor of mankind. The struggle of Christ with his enemy has shifted back to the political sphere. The individual Christian and the Christian congregation always stand between Christ and Counter-Christ. But where is that? Käsemann tries to specify: "For the first time in remembered history the tide is running against us, and for the first time since the early days of Christianity it is possible seriously to imagine that the vision of the Book of Revelation is literally being fulfilled: that the Antichrist is enthroned visibly and universally on the graves of the saints and only in the desert is there room for the people of God."[42]

There are many who would question the wisdom of reviving the juxtaposing rhetoric of apocalyptic: God and Satan, the divine and the demonic, good and evil, heaven and hell, life and death, cross and resurrection, etc. Instead, we prefer the nonpolarizing myth of the middle way, the golden mean, the grayish blending of black and white. Surely there is good reason to be suspicious of the symbols of apocalypse, insofar as they have also been the playthings of eschatological sharp-shooters, gazing into the distant future, and producing unreal agendas of "last things." That is eschatology as futuristic historicism; it deserves to be relegated to an appendix of Christian dogmatics, where Schleiermacher always put the things he didn't believe. It must be made unmistakably clear that those who reappropriate apocalyptic images have not the slightest interest in drawing aside the veil that separates the known present from the unknown future. It is, rather, a question of having symbols that match the realities of the present. For after all, why does the imagination reach for symbols of the future? The answer is: in order to reveal the present in its imperfection, its transitoriness, and its convertibility. The present is not what it ought to be; it is in motion, and can even be changed into something quite other. The images of the future intend to grasp that other dimension which the present is lacking. The image of the new man, the ultra-human, the coming Son of Man, catches the reflection of man who now exists, and reveals him as less than human, in Ray Hart's phrase, as "unfinished man." The symbols of the future picture alternatives, and in this way they open the way for self-transcending in the present. Wherever the symbols of the future are contracted into the realities of the present, man's imagination has become crippled and his society stagnant, no matter how fast new models pass in and out of existence. So it is with the apocalyptic symbols; they divide one's perceptions; they split the world; things do not merely run together; they are antithetical. There is no Christ alone; he establishes his identity in relation to the Counter-Christ. There is no gospel as such; it can be known only where the law has worked its full measure of misery; there is nothing holy except that which is distinctly set apart from the profane. In Hegelian terms this means that the negativity that belongs to the nature of every finite thing is necessarily linked with its opposite. Similarly, in the Gospels it is the demon-possessed who are able to recognize the Christ.

In Jewish apocalyptic there is a constant struggle going on between God and Satan. At times this struggle is portrayed as occurring outside of history, in the air, so to speak. It is this impression that caused von Rad to say that apocalyptic bears no existential relation to history. In Christian apocalyptic the divine and demonic forces are made internal to history on account of the incarnational motif.[43] God and Satan are carrying out their battle through their incarnate forms in history: Christ and Counter-Christ. There is a christological reduction of the apocalyptic symbolism, so that it can be placed strictly at the service of history. If this symbolism should disappear from the missionary consciousness of the church, the church would lose its power to combat the demonries of the present, to confront the agencies of the Counter-Christ with the exorcizing function of the gospel. So the church looks at its environing society in terms of problems, needs, weaknesses, and injustices, and rushes in with help to ameliorate the situation, but it is impotent to touch the great forces that move underneath the social surface. When it has no arousing name for anything, it can neither isolate nor attack any of the present structures of evil. The church today is sparring against "flesh and blood" and does not sense itself in mortal combat against "principalities and powers." Otherwise it would not remain silent in face of the demonic structures on which American society is based.

In 1926 Paul Tillich wrote a prophetic article entitled. "The Concept of the Demonic and Its Meaning for Systematic Theology."[44] That was greeted by Rudolf Bultmann with astonishment, since at the same time he was getting ready to demythologize all the gruesome symbols of the apocalypse. What kind of a primitive mind is it that would revive such a relic of ancient mythology? Tillich's counterattack was to the effect that demythologizing can be a tool of bourgeois Christianity, which is willing to exchange the socially agressive and politically aggravating symbols for a hyphenated form of relation with culture. Culture-Christianity dissolves the transcendent symbols that work within history to resist the status quo actively. Since the Enlightenment the list of forbidden symbols has been growing. Particularly, the historical symbols that can split the realities in the social and political sphere have all been dissolved by the glow of positivistic rationality or by the device of demythologizing which brings about the introversion of apocalyptic.

There are a few faint glimpses of hope that the negative principle of apocalyptic is making a comeback in contemporary theology. Unfortunately, no theologian has yet followed up the lead that Tillich gave in his creative interpretation of the concept of the demonic, his key principle in the interpretation of history. On the other end of the Continent there was Nicholas Berdyaev, somewhat a loner, whose insight into present realities was nourished by the symbols of Christian apocalypse. Today, the principle of Counter-Christ appears in the writings of Moltmann, Alves, and Altizer, in quite various expressions. Alves writes about "the dynamics of the politics of the Anti-Christ, the one who wants to kill the Messiah, the presence of the future."[45] The politics of the Antichrist is the politics of domination, oppression, slavery; the politics of the Christ stands in opposition to the principalities, the world rulers of this present darkness, the spiritual hosts of wickedness (Eph. 6:12). Or does anyone imagine that the realities to which these symbols point have somehow lost any of their ruthless power in modern times? I think there is a problem in the way in which both Moltmann and Altizer have worked out and applied their principle of negation. Moltmann's idea of *inadaequatio rei et intellectus*[46] and Altizer's idea that apocalyptic religion reverses all meaning, value, and identity would literally demolish the proleptic eschatology on which the Christian message is founded.[47] Both of them mean, however, in spite of all dualistic antitheses, that the new creation is born through the negation of the old, and is not its mere replacement. The rebirth of the negative consciousness in modern theology, traceable back to biblical apocalyptic, is a healthy sign that although we may be standing on the edge of apocalypse, the gospel can come alive today to equip the saints to survive the fire and the judgment, to do battle with the dragon and the beast. Mood-wise, we are going to have a kind of rerun of the theology of crisis, although the dialetic will be different, since it will not go from above to below, but from the future to the present, for the sake of mediating the new into history, and creating a new tomorrow through revolutionary transformation of the world.

## NOTES

1. See the *Journal for Theology and the Church*, ed. by Robert W. Funk, Vol. 6, entitled *Apocalypticism* (New York: Herder and Herder, 1969). See also Wolfhart Pannenberg, *et al.*, *Revelation as History* (New York: Macmillan Company, 1968); Klaus Koch, *Ratlos vor der Apokalyptik*, which was not available to me at the time of this writing.

2. For a book-length treatment of this thesis, see August Strobel, *Kerygma und Apokalyptik* (Göttingen: Vandenhoeck & Ruprecht, 1967).

3. See Gerhard Ebeling's dialogue with Rudolf Bultmann, *Theology and Proclamation* (Philadelphia: Fortress Press, 1966).

4. Rudolf Bultmann, "The Primitive Christian Kerygma and the Historical Jesus," *The Historical Jesus and the Kerygmatic Christ*, ed. by Carl E. Braaten and Roy A. Harrisville (Nashville: Abingdon Press, 1967), pp. 15-42.

5. Ernst Käsemann, "The Beginnings of Christian Theology," *Journal for Theology and the Church, op. cit.,* pp. 17-46; *New Testament Questions of Today* (Philadelphia: Fortress Press, 1969), pp. 82-107.

6. I am assuming that a successful apologetic must take seriously the particularities of both the original horizon within which the message occurred and the contemporary horizon within which it has to happen again. That is, the criteria of identity, continuity, and contemporaneity are indispensable to sound apologetic theology.

7. The evidence for the truth of this assertion may be found in Paul Tillich, *The Interpretation of History* (New York: Charles Scribner's Sons, 1936).

8. Ernst Käsemann, "On the Topic of Primitive Christian Apocalytic," *Journal for Theology and the Church, op. cit.,* p. 100. *New Testament Questions of Today, op. cit.,* p. 109.

9. *Ibid.*, p. 100.

10. *Ibid.*, p. 100, n. 1; in *New Testament Questions of Today*, p. 109, n. 1.

11. *Ibid.*, p. 107, n. 5; in *New Testament Questions of Today*, p. 115, n. 8.

12. See Ernst Bloch's, *Atheismus im Christentum. Zur Religion des Exodus und des Reichs* (Frankfurt/Main: Suhrkamp Verlag, 1968).

13. Gerhard Ebeling, "The Ground of Christian Theology," *Journal for Theology and the Church, op. cit.*, p. 51.

14. Ernst Käsemann, "On the Topic of Primitive Christian Apocalyptic," *op. cit.*, pp. 107, n. 5; 115, n. 8.

15. Ernst Käsemann, "The Beginnings of Christian Theology," *op. cit.*, pp. 40; 101.

16. Ulrich Wilkens, "The Understanding of Revelation Within the History of Primitive Christianity," *Revelation as History, op. cit.*, pp. 57-121.

17. See the important book on apocalyptic and law by Dietrich Rössler, *Gesetz und Geschichte* (Neukirchener Verlag, 1960).

18. Hans Dieter Betz misconstrues the facts when he alleges that Ulrich Wilkens portrays Jesus as an apocalypticist. On the contrary, Wilkens explicitly teaches that Jesus was not an apocalypticist, although the context within which Jesus established his unique identity was determined by apocalyptic thought forms. See the very inaccurate essay on the Pannenberg group by Hans Dieter Betz, "The Concept of Apocalyptic in the Theology of Pannenberg," *Journal for Theology and the Church, op. cit.*, pp. 192-207.

19. Gerhard Ebeling is right in his insistence that for Christian faith Jesus' modification of apocalyptic is the important thing. "We do not by any means merely interpret Jesus in the light of apocalyptic, but also and above all apocalyptic in the light of Jesus" ("The Ground of Christian Theology," *op. cit.*, p. 58).

20. In the section on apocalyptic in the revised edition of his *Theologie des Alten Testaments,* von Rad states that "we do not really know what the nature of apocalypticism is" (4th German ed. [1965], pp. 315f.).

21. Oscar Cullmann, *Salvation in History* (London: SCM Press, 1967), p. 83.

22. Gerhard von Rad, *Old Testament Theology*, Vol. II (New York: Harper & Row, 1965), pp. 303, 304.

23. Hans Dieter Betz, "On the Problem of the Religio-Historical Understanding of Apocalypticism," *Journal for Theology and the Church, op. cit.*, p. 138.

24. Gerhard von Rad seems to have hit upon this idea, but failed to make anything of it. He states: "The characteristic of apocalyptic theology is its eschatological dualism, the clear-cut differentiation of two aeons, the present one and the one to come" (*Old Testament Theology,* II, pp. 301-302) .

25. H. H. Rowley, *The Relevance of Apocalyptic* (London: Lutterworth Press, 1944) , p. 174.

26. The most thorough characterization of apocalyptic appears in Johann Michael Schmidt, *Die jüdische Apokalyptik. Die Geschichte ihrer Erforschung von den Anfängen bis zu den Textfunden von Qumran* (Neukirchener Verlag, 1969) .

27. Karl Rahner, "The Hermeneutics of Eschatological Assertions," *Theological Investigations,* Vol. IV (Baltimore: Helicon Press, 1966) , p. 337. Edward Schillebeeckx has stumbled onto the same path as Rahner in his handling of eschatology as extrapolation. Thus: "The post-terrestrial *eschaton* is but a question of the manner in which what is already growing in the history of this world will receive its final fulfillment." ("The Interpretation of Eschatology," *Concilium,* Vol. 41, *The Problem of Eschatology,* ed. by Edward Schillebeeckx [Paramus, N.J.: Paulist Press, 1969], p. 53). In distinct contrast to these views, Jürgen Moltmann distinguishes the "theology of hope" of Thomas Aquinas, "which is actually an ontology of desire" from his own "eschatological theology which wants to appropriate and develop the apocalyptic thought forms of the New Testament." He makes other illuminating comparisons: "If K. Rahner in the dialogue with Marxism calls God 'the absolute future,' and Teilhard de Chardin in dialogue with science talks about 'Point Omega,' the question arises as to whether God appears as extrapolation and convergence point of all movement in the world or whether one anticipates the *Deus adventurus* in the contradictory movement of the world and thus provokes contradiction to the negative." ("Theology as Eschatology," in *The Future of Hope,* edited by Frederick Herzog [New York: Herder and Herder, 1970], p. 13, n. 19.)

28. Reflections on the difference between development and liberation have achieved their clearest expression in Mr. Ivan Illich's Center in Cuernavaca, Mexico. See his collection of writings, *The Church, Change and Development* (Chicago: Urban Training Center Press, 1970) . He no longer appears to be using the concept of development in as positive a sense as occurs generally in these writings. His next book of essays, titled *Celebration of Awareness: A Call for Institutional Revolution* (Garden City: Doubleday & Company, 1970) , underscores more clearly the problem inherent in the concept of development, especially as it applies to the Latin American situation.

29. Rudolf Bultmann, *Jesus and the Word* (New York: Charles Scribner's Sons, 1934) , p. 51.

30. *Ibid.,* p. 158.

31. See my discussion on these two words in *The Future of God* (New York: Harper & Row, 1969) , pp. 29-30. Also Gerhard Sauter, "The Future: A Question for the Christian-Marxist Dialogue," in *Concilium,* 41, *op. cit.,* p. 131.

32. Herbert Marcuse, *One Dimensional Man* (London: Routledge & Kegan Paul, 1964) .

33. See Ernst Käsemann's polemic, *Jesus Means Freedom* (Philadelphia: Fortress Press, 1970) .

34. See Karl Jaspers' discussion of the idea of *coincidentia oppositorum* in *Philosophical Faith and Revelation* (London: Collins, 1967) , pp. 259ff.

35. See Herbert Marcuse's study of Hegel and Marx, *Reason and Revolution,* in which the negative principle is fully elaborated (Boston: Beacon Press, 1960; esp. pp. 65, 123, 141ff.) . Marcuse writes as a modern philosopher of revolution who, unlike his fellow intellectual Ernst Bloch, masks the apocalyptic origins of his thought forms, particularly his appeal to two-dimensional thinking.

36. "Hegel's dialectic is permeated with the profound conviction that all immediate forms of existence—in nature and history—are 'bad,' because they do not permit things to be what they can be. True existence begins only when the immediate state is recognized as negative, when beings become 'subjects' and strive to adapt their outward state to their potentialities." (Herbert Marcuse, *Reason and Revolution,* p. 66.) The apocalyptic negation of reality must be distinguished from gnostic-Manichaean dualism, on the ground of its radical monotheism. To say with Hegel that everything is "bad" is not meant in an absolute sense; that would be Manichaean. Rather, it is only bad relatively, i.e., relative to the good into which it is destined to pass through negation.

37. See his chapter, "Der Gott der Hoffnung," in *Ernst Bloch zu ehren,* ed. by Siegfried Unseld (Frankfurt/Main: Suhrkamp Verlag, 1965) , pp. 209ff.

38. With the sixteenth-century Reformers I do not use this term to refer to an individual figure, but to a power structure.

39. Note what Tillich writes: "The symbol most impressive for our time, comprehending the final depth of holy demonry, is the 'Grand Inquisitor,' as Dostoievsky visualized and placed him opposite Christ: the religion which makes itself absolute and therefore must destroy the saint in whose name it is established—the demonic will to power of

the sacred institution" (*The Interpretation of History* [New York: Charles Scribner's Sons, 1936], p. 80).

40. See Josef Ernst, *Die eschatologischen Gegenspieler in den Schriften des Neuen Testaments* (Regensburg: Verlag Friedrich Pustet, 1967).

41. See Hans Preuss, *Die Vorstellungen vom Antichrist im späteren Mittelalter, bei Luther und in der konfessionellen Polemik* (Leipzig: J. C. Hinrichs'sche Buchhandlung, 1906).

42. Ernst Käsemann, "Theologians and Laity," *New Testament Questions for Today* (Philadelphia: Fortress Press, 1969), p. 288.

43. Jakob Taubes has traced how the transcendent symbols of ancient apocalyptic became progressively and massively internalized in the course of Western history, in *Abendländische Eschatologie* (Berlin: A. Francke Ag. Verlag, 1947). In my opinion, the significance of this book has been neglected in the contemporary discussions on eschatology.

44. In *Offenbarung und Glaube, Gesammelte Werke*, Vol. VIII (Stuttgart: Evangelisches Verlagswerk, 1970), pp. 285-291.

45. Rubem A. Alves, *A Theology of Human Hope* (Washington: Corpus Books, 1969), p. 114.

46. Jürgen Moltmann, *Theology of Hope* (London: SCM Press, 1967), pp. 85, 118.

47. Thomas J. J. Altizer, *The Descent into Hell* (Philadelphia: J. B. Lippincott, 1970), esp. Chap. 2, "The Kingdom of God."

# 2

# The Future
# as the Source
# of Freedom

## A Hermeneutic of Liberation

"Freedom" is one of the great words in Christianity. It is also the strongest impulse in humanity. What is the connection between the Christian word and the human impulse? My answer to this question will be set forth in this chapter as a kind of micro-synthesis of trends in modern theology and culture. It is notoriously difficult to achieve a synthesis of any kind; but I want to suggest that if we can catch the thread of freedom, we might be able to tie together a lot of things in theology that seem extraneous, disjointed, and even antagonistic.

In the New Testament field we have run the gamut from the problem of demythologizing to the new quest of the historical Jesus to the new hermeneutics and now to the recovery of apocalyptic eschatology—four shifts of interest and approach in the course of two decades. In the Old Testament field we were all awakened from our biblicist slumbers by the documentary hypothesis, but after that we were simply at a loss how to choose from among the many channels of interpretation. Always a major problem was that of finding one hermeneutical backbone that could keep the two parts of the Bible together in the same body of faith. Here we are going to suggest that the unity of the two Testaments can be grasped best by a hermeneutic of liberation that reads the history of Israel as the story of freedom that reaches its dénouement with the ingression of the eschatological future of God in the man Jesus of Nazareth.

If we turn to the fields of historical and systematic theology, we can be helped here too if we can catch the thread of freedom. Much of contemporary theology has been a kind of neo-Reformation synthesis. Neo-Orthodoxy was a misnomer from the beginning. The dominant brands of Protestant theology after World War I—the Barths, Brunners, and Niebuhrs—were versions of the Ritschlian hermeneutic, namely, back to the Bible by way of the Reformation. This neo-Reformation synthesis was what kept the historical and systematic theologians on common ground. Lundensian theology offers us the most extreme example. The systematic mode of reflection disappeared altogether in motif-research. One had only to trace a motif—the central religious motif—from the Bible up to its purest historical expression in the "young man Luther." Our grip on this neo-Reformation theology, that seemed so much alive just after World War II, has been gradually slipping. Without a new horizon of interpretation we are now in danger of falling into a posture of discontinuity, thereby surrendering the achievements of the great scholars and theologians who collaborated in the renaissance of the Reformation. I take it for granted that we need a new horizon broad enough to encompass the old insights without merely repeating them. The drive to freedom makes such a new horizon possible. This has the best chance of forging new links between the ferment of liberation in our world today and the outburst of freedom in Luther's preaching of the gospel. We can go back to Luther without ceasing to be modern only if his pointings continue to move us closer to the zone of freedom.

This same horizon of freedom can place the historical study of the Bible in direct continuity with, and at the service of, theological interpretations of modern culture. Dogmatic theology has become a cul-de-sac in most Christian traditions. It has not really been open to the modern historical study of the Bible. For the most part it has reshuffled traditional doctrines, to which more and more biblical study is prepared to offer less and less support. And dogmatic theology has been equally well sealed off from what is stirring in its environing culture. For these reasons dogmatic theology hardly exists today. It seems to me to be an anachronism even in its militantly self-conscious Barthian form. Nevertheless, continuity is important here too, and it can be had only by recasting the meaning of dogma. Dogmas are not atoms of divinity in history; they are not pieces of the divine mind in the church; they are not revealed propositions of eternal validity. Rather, they are signals of meaning in the history of freedom, and therefore vibrations of the Transcendent Future. A dogma is not a truth in itself but only a verbal pointing to events that are animated by the spirit of freedom. In this way the doctrine of the church can be related to the broader cultural currents, for freedom is the motor power of culture.

It was the Italian philosopher, Benedetto Croce, who dusted off a page from Hegel's forgotten philosophy of history and told us that "history is the history of liberty" and "liberty is the eternal creator of history and itself the subject of every history."[1] Croce thus designated freedom as the "explanatory principle of the course of history."[2] I think he learned that from the Bible, even though he could not see the finger of God in the course of human events that gave birth to freedom. And he could not see that the liberation process in history is the vehicle of divine promise for still greater freedom—for the eschatological liberty of the children of God (Rom. 8:21).

The hermeneutic of liberation cannot merely be a historical pathway into the Bible as a collection of documents reporting the early beginnings and development of freedom in history. It has the broader task of encompassing the question of God. The hermeneutic of liberation is both historical and theological; it is the method of a theology of history as the story of freedom. The renewal of God-language must occur within the horizon of freedom, if such language is to make real sense under the conditions of modern subjectivity.[3] For the atheistic criticism of God-language has been motivated not so much by an anti-theism as by a passion for freedom. I do not believe any doctrine of God is viable even for Christians today which does not take up the truth of the atheistic criticism in a dialectical way, that is, without finding a better theological way of sponsoring and augmenting the drive toward freedom that is the positive factor underlying the negativities of modern atheism.[4]

We cannot forget that atheism was born in the West, on Christian soil, in German universities, and, as Tillich used to remind us, especially in Lutheran parsonages. Atheism has found fertile soil in the guts of preachers' kids. They have had to stage rebellions on behalf of freedom within the authoritarian atmosphere of the parsonage and of the church. So they have had to get rid of the God who was created in their fathers' image. If atheism is the allergy of a faith that hates idolatry because idolatry is the acutest form of slavery, then the only antidote is to picture God as the liberator of mankind, as the very source of freedom itself. That is the picture we can get from the Bible if we read it as the history of the gospel of freedom.

## THE STORY OF FREEDOM IN THE BIBLE

*A. Israel.* The entire story of freedom in the Bible is told against the background of the liberation of Israel from slavery in Egypt. The war of liberation was planned and executed by the God of freedom. It was a political act that projected Israel, a tiny slave people, into the openness of world history. There they have been visible and vulnerable, the subjects of pogroms and genocide. The fact that they have survived at all may be the best proof around that God is alive.[5] The blood of freedom has been drawn from their veins to quench the thirst of a long line of tyrants—the Pharaohs, Caesars, Czars,

and Hitlers. And sad to say, Christians have often been the
most willing oppressors of the children of Abraham.

How did it happen that Israel should be chosen to bear
the torch of freedom and thus influence the course of world
history? The answer, I think, lies in Israel's imageless image
of God. All of Yahweh's contemporary rivals in Egypt,
Canaan, Babylonia, Persia, and Rome could be replicated in
plastic images. An image is static, but Yahweh is dynamic.
An image can be manipulated like a dead object, but Yahweh
is the living voice of the future. Yahweh's secret to survival
was the fact that he had both his freedom and his future in
himself. The other gods were decked out with myths about
their origins (theogony). But Yahweh was the unoriginated
One, coming out of nowhere and out of nothing. He was a
new God that appeared to Israel out of the unknown future
in an act of pre-eminent freedom, and he said, "I will be your
God, and you will be my people." When people ask who sent
you, say, "Yahweh—I will be who I will be," that is, the very
Future of Reality and the Source of Freedom "has sent me"
(Exod. 3:14). I believe Pannenberg has drawn out the significance of this utterance, although in language a bit more
speculative than the Hebrews were used to: "The very idea
of God demands that there be no future beyond himself. He
is the ultimate future. This in turn suggests that God should
be conceived as pure freedom. For what is freedom but to
have future in oneself and out of oneself?"[6]

The modern existentialist idea that the heart of freedom
is openness to the future has its original ground in Israel's
experience of a God whose futurity cancels the finality of
every existing image and every past or present apprehension.
Historical life is based on promise, on a covenant that is
freely initiated and mutually agreed upon. Life is drawn out
of the encirclement of a closed cosmos and projected into the
openness of an unfinished history. There is no firm foothold
in history, for each day the people of God have to touch
down in a new situation of events through which God is free
to act on the spur of the moment. Israel is never able to pin

God down. And as we shall see when we deal with Jesus' radicalization of God's freedom, not even the law which comes from God can usurp the freedom to transcend its boundaries. That is the freedom of grace.

Israel's religion of freedom exercised its power in a negative and in a positive way. Negatively, we see it in the process of demythologizing. If modern men think they find too much myth in the Old Testament, to Israel's pagan contemporaries there was by far not enough. To use current jargon, Israel historicized the myths, so that the battle of the gods in heaven was made internal to the struggle of human affairs in history. While there was no complete demythologizing, the available myths were so bent out of shape as to be made a shambles from the point of view of the surrounding religions. Giving priority to the covenants of history brought liberation from the enslaving power of myth and magic, from astral forces and orgiastic cults.

Positively, the religion of freedom took an ethico-political turn in the preaching of the prophets. A dialectical interpretation of history is Israel's greatest gift to political understanding. The prophet of Israel had a magnificent vision of the future as a realm of peace and justice and truth and fullness. One could say, "So what?" about all this utopianism, but this becomes the trigger mechanism for a one-sided engagement in the course of human events. The prophet attacks those men and structures that are now living in reverse of God's future. He knows that the established rituals of religion and the honored codes of morality have become the chains that kings and priests and rich men use to keep the masses in bondage. The prophet is a theologian of history who sees that it is the little people at the bottom who are God's levers of liberation. So he sides with the revolutionary opposition using his voice and muscle in behalf of the poor, the oppressed, and the useless little people in the world. The black theologian James Cone has caught the meaning of this dialectical one-sidedness for our time. He has said, "God has made an unqualified identification with the black people.

Either God is for the black people in their fight for liberation and against the white oppressors or he is not. He cannot be both for us and for white people at the same time." The church paper reporting this called it "a new theological view."[7] But it's really not so new. It's quite old, not as old as creation, but as old as the prophets.

The paradigm of the prophetic imagination was Israel's own election. A little tribe of Bedouin nomads was chosen to be exalted above all nations. A group of runaway slaves, a bunch of hungry children in the desert, men and women huddling in ghettos—they were chosen to lead the way of liberation for all men and nations. Jesus said, "Salvation is of the Jews" (John 4:22) .

*B. Jesus.* As Christians we can literally say that salvation is of the Jews, because Jesus was a Jew. The salvation he brings is freedom, and happily this is recognized in the title of Käsemann's latest book, *Jesus Means Freedom.*[8]

The freedom which Jesus lived had its source in the kingdom which he brought. The inbreaking of the kingdom takes hold in history by the freeing of slaves. A slave is anyone who is in bondage to powers that stand in the way of the coming of the rule of pure freedom. The power of Jesus' freedom is eschatological, but the place of its realization is history. Käsemann poses the question: "Was Jesus a liberal?"[9] He answers that "the gospels do not leave us in the slightest doubt that Jesus, judged by the standards of his religious environment, was in fact 'liberal.' "[10] How far a tradition has strayed from the freedom of Jesus and that glorious liberty of the children of God when the word "liberal" has become a searing iron to brand the enemy! Jesus had a liberal attitude; his openness to the future of God's kingdom placed him above Moses and the Scriptures themselves. Love broke through the canons of orthodoxy to give some free room to those who couldn't pay the rent to stay inside the current social setup. Jesus was an extremist for freedom because love would have it no other way. Jesus is God as the incarnation of love, and therefore of pure freedom, seeking nothing else but the enjoyment of free love. Paul, the apostle of Jesus, makes the claim that it was "for freedom Christ has set us free" (Gal. 5:1) .

Freedom is not a means to an end, as in the standard brands of orthodoxy. Freedom is the end itself, because God is pure freedom. Therefore freedom is not a psychological state that makes it possible to enjoy resubmitting oneself to the law. The law is given only because of sin, but where freedom reigns there is no law, because the law has been absorbed by freedom in such a way that ultimately there is only the "law of liberty" (James 1:25 and 2:12) . By that we shall be judged, because love will have it no other way. Love is the substance of freedom, and freedom the substance of love. They can be defined only in terms of each other. But law trails far behind as merely an emergency measure in case of the backfiring of love and freedom. I like what Käsemann says: "Freedom can never be carried to excess; it can always be inadequately represented."[11]

The only limit to Christian freedom is Jesus himself. But that is felt as no restriction, because Jesus is the medium of freedom. Jesus means freedom because he is the risen Lord as the man of the cross. The cross is the acid test of freedom. Every humanistic idea of freedom comes up short in front of the cross because it cannot deal with the future of death. Only that man is free who is not hung up on his own dying, who can live as though death itself is dead. If nothing but the future of death can be projected back into existence by the anticipating imagination, then the most a man can have is a "dreadful freedom" that turns his hope to despair. Paradoxically, the man who has come to terms with his death in the dying of Christ has found life, even though he is lying on his deathbed. With that statement we have touched the mystery of absolute freedom for which our best symbols (immortality and resurrection) are like sighings of the Spirit too deep for utterance (Rom. 8:26) .

## THE DRIVE TO FREEDOM IN ATHEISM

If the Bible is the story of liberty, why is it that often those who study it the most have the hardest time practicing it? I cannot answer that, but I know the answer lies close to the heart of what we call "sin." Paul states, "Where the Spirit of the Lord is, there is freedom." And what is sin but striving against the Spirit? Käsemann charges that "freedom is no longer the mighty river, carrying the whole life of the Christian and the church, but just a trickle."[12] At some point in history, perhaps with the beginning of the Constantinian era, the spirit of freedom in Christianity gave way to the spirit of the Grand Inquisitor. The history of Christianity is the tragedy of freedom. The inquisitorial spirit has forced some of the best minds and the purest souls to leave the church to join a company of freer men. How odd that "free-thinking" should become a dirty term in a religion which calls men to freedom (Gal. 5:13) and teaches that truth alone can make men free (John 8:32). The very meaning of being in the truth involves being there freely. Whenever truth is coerced, it turns into its exact opposite in human subjectivity. Realizing this, Kierkegaard maintained that "subjectivity is truth."

Whenever it happened that the spirit of freedom had to find its patrons outside the church, a wedge was driven between freedom and God. Then God ascended to the pinnacle of all the powers that collaborate to hold freedom down. The dominant picture of God in Western orthodoxy, whether Roman or Protestant, has been as the foremost advocate of law and order. Man is a low-down sniveling slave who must carry out the orders of an autocratic ruler sitting on a throne high above. But a sovereign ruler exacting blind obedience to his will and authority can only stir up a strong desire to be rid of such a relationship for the sake of freedom. Faith in freedom is a stronger and more deserving passion than obedience to authority. A religion of law and order is the cult of Caesar; when it is carried into the church, it becomes the tyranny of the Antichrist. But the Spirit of Christ presses on for the triumph of greater love and freedom.

We can understand atheism as a revolution of freedom against the idea of God as the ultimate source of authoritarian relations in society. The slavish mentality among Christians that so nauseated Nietzsche can be traced to the picture of God as absolute legislator. Belief in God as the last sanction of the established world order was diagnosed as the root cause of the pathology of slavish social relations. To accelerate the struggle for freedom, it was necessary to proclaim the "death of God." The positive message of the "death-of-God" movement since Nietzsche and Jean Paul[13] deals with a new self-understanding of man. If by definition God must be experienced in the depths of human existence, then any change in these depths will bring about a corresponding change in man's experience of God. It is not God who is dead, but only certain modes of apprehending his presence and certain ways of imaging his reality.

The meaning of the word "God" cannot be explored by itself as a naked vocable. To affirm or to deny the existence of God, as well as to reserve one's judgment about the matter, is all quite meaningless apart from the human corollary. Further, what one affirms or denies about God always contains a hidden conviction about man. Luther said that God is where you put your heart. "A god is that to which we look for all good and in which we find refuge in every time of need. To have a god is nothing else than to trust and believe him with our whole heart. As I have often said, the trust and faith of the heart alone make both God and an idol. If your faith and trust are right, then your God is the true God. On the other hand, if your trust is false and wrong, then you have not the true God. For these two belong together, faith and God. That to which your heart clings and entrusts itself is, I say, really your God."[14] The point of this quotation is to help express something fundamental on the way to a postatheistic doctrine of God. As the depths of the heart go, so goes the image we have of God. If there are no depths, there is no God. That is, no God appears. Therefore, we should not be surprised at how widespread atheism is.

There is a vulgar sort of atheism—an atheism of vulgar minds which have no depth. They may be among the peasants or the Ph.D.s; what we usually call "getting an education" has little to do with "spirit" and "soul" and "depth," with the inner space in man. I do not wish to deal with the problem of vulgar atheism. There is nothing new or promising about it. The chief difference between now and former times on this score is that today we have statistics and communications to make us aware of the extent of vulgar atheism in the world. However, there is another kind of atheism that reaches its position of anti-theism with great sensitivity to the dimension of depth in human subjectivity. We are using the term "subjectivity" as the modern equivalent of Luther's concept of "heart," which he derived from the Bible.

In the inner dimension of subjectivity man has been in quest of himself. But what does it mean to be in quest of one's self or to search for one's identity? It is hard to say, for we have the story of this quest mostly in negative terms. It is the story of man's freedom from whatever he has experienced as enslaving, negating, or repressive. Every major step toward freedom since the Middle Ages has been mistaken for atheism by people in authority. The rise of modern science was opposed by orthodox churchmen and theologians. But what was happening was that man was freeing himself from cosmocentric metaphysics and authoritarian religion, from life that merely seesawed between necessity and authority. God as the numinous halo around the world, as a fixed order in which there was a ready-made slot for man, had to be denied to make room for freedom and newness.

On another front existentialism ended in atheism in order to give expression to the boundlessness of human freedom. The essences of reality had to be negated because they were clamps that restricted the range of freedom. The slogan "existence precedes essence" meant that even God has to be negated as an objectively existing entity because he would cramp the style of human freedom. This means, I think, that unless we wish to reject the existentialist cry that is born out of freedom, we shall have to show that God is not *per definitionem* the outside limit of human freedom, but its very ground and meaning.[15] Existentialism would not have had to become anti-theistic if theism had not become an absolutist ideology opposing the freedom of man.

Existentialism is a less potent form of atheism than Marxism; however, both of them can be answered only when to speak of God is to speak better of freedom, for Marxism is a cry for liberation.[16] Marxism calls for liberation from the alienating forms of life which man has created on top of the world of nature. Atheism does not seem to be a *fundamental* doctrine of Marxism, except as the antithesis to a God who is pictured as the original creator and guarantor of the social and economic systems that enslave and oppress. Within the context of a theism that has allied itself with capitalism and the so-called "free-world," the Marxist concern for liberation is driven to a posture of anti-theism and revolutionary communism. The tragedy of Marxism is that its concern for one kind of liberation has lured men into other forms of slavery, and it is oblivious of its own captivity to oppressive forms of thinking and acting.

Today's counter-culture, in contrast, is seeking to regain or to attain a vision of freedom[17] that goes deeper than Christianity and Marxism and that bears unmistakable likeness to the freedom dreams in the apocalyptic portions of the Bible. The leading spokesmen for a counter-culture believe in the ultimate value of freedom; they have an ontology of freedom and an ethic of freedom; but they renege a theology of freedom and a religion of freedom. The doctrine of God seems to be not only irrelevant but even obstructive to the works and ways of freedom.

## GOD AS THE LIBERATOR OF MANKIND

It is a scandal that in the so-called Christian West men should posit the freedom they seek outside the being of God. When a wedge is driven between freedom and God, men must choose freedom rather than God. This is a real dilemma, but a false one. It is real, because in actuality men have been confronted with a God who opposes the freedom they seek. But it is a false one, because the essence of God who is really God is nothing other than that freedom which man is seeking when he is in search of the truth and reality of his own identity. Atheism that has arisen as a protest for freedom can be overcome when the freedom man lacks has its source in God. In going ahead to freedom, man is approaching freedom's source in God. Man is bound to seek freedom because he is not yet free to be. Only God is free to be because the reality he enjoys is underived freedom as such.

Christianity in the West separated the stream of freedom from its source in the Spirit of God when the doctrine of the grace of God was opposed to the freedom of man. The doctrine of God's grace is miserably formulated whenever it is contrasted with the free will of man. For then free will is thought of as something man already has in competition with the grace of God. Who wants grace if to gain it one must lose his freedom? Free will is not a natural attribute of man which exists in competition with grace. Freedom is self-determination in the inner depths of one's being, but this is precisely what man does not have in and of himself. It is a gift of grace.

Freedom is what grace gives, and not what grace meets in man as its rival. Grace is the power of salvation as freedom. Man is free when he is open beyond himself. He is not free when he is sealing himself off from the source of freedom in the power of the future beyond himself. By turning in upon himself he may think he is in possession of himself, and therefore free, but in actuality he is imprisoned in what he already is, determined by the sum total of his past history. To be free is to be open to the future, to find the reality of one's freedom in the oncoming future of God. The reality of God is the power of the future which opens man to new possibilities and supports him in the very act of his freedom.

Grace is not opposed to freedom, but is its very ground and resource. With this insight it would be necessary to reevaluate the history of grace and of freedom that runs through the great controversies between Augustine and Pelagius, Luther and Erasmus, Jansenists and Molinists, etc. One cannot dismiss either side. The problem was so badly put that the defenders of grace sounded like denigrators of human freedom. On the other hand, it must not be forgotten that precisely those who denied free will for the sake of grace— for example, Luther and the Jansenists—were more vigorous in their defense of the liberty of the Christian man over against the church's authority than either Erasmus or the Jesuits. One could generalize even further and say that while Roman Catholic theology has championed free will more vigorously than Protestantism, considering the latter's emphasis on *sola gratia,* it has been less arduous in support of the freedom of conscience. What it has given with one hand it has withdrawn with the other. These confusions have been tolerated on both sides because of an underdeveloped and sometmes even erroneous theology of freedom.

The human quest for freedom is infinite, because every condition of life, even at its very best, is experienced as a lack. One of Berdyaev's friends once remarked that Leibniz must have been the world's greatest pessimist; Leibniz thought this was the best of all possible worlds.[18] But if this is the best possible world, what would the bad ones look like? Such a pessimism is denied by life itself, which goes forward to new and fresh forms of freedom.

The experience of God always includes the dimension of transcendence. Transcendence can be conceptualized in different ways. The experience of reaching out beyond every limit in the present toward a fuller freedom of life is the form under which modern man can experience the transcendence of God today.[19] God is experienced as the power of liberation. If God is pictured as the liberator of mankind, luring men beyond every kind of bondage under an existing set of facts, there is psychologically no longer any need to opt for atheism for the sake of freedom. God is the power who supports man in the struggle for freedom. He is the sustaining ground of hope for liberation. The transcendence of God is experienced as the *élan vital* that opens toward the fullness of life in the mystery of God's personal freedom. The doctrine of the Trinity is an expression of the interior richness of that fullness, infinitely transcending the immobilism of a static unity.

The idea of God as the ground and source of freedom can help the church to take new initiatives in the present struggles of mankind for liberation. It is a shame on Christianity that perhaps the boldest initiatives for freedom today are being taken by atheistic revolutionaries. Christian revolutionaries are few and far between, and some of these are in an identity crisis, unsure of their theological ground. Often they might feel as though they have more in common with their atheistic co-revolutionaries than with their fellow Christians who are more interested in keeping order than in winning new freedoms for others. The essence of the black revolution and student radicalism is the drive toward freedom. Now, the gospel is the promise of liberation.

When Christians show with their lives that the freedom which Jesus means is an invitation to participate in the liberation movements in the world, these movements will be purged of their tendencies toward atheistic thought and violent action. The freedom that is the heart of the Christian vision of the future is the freedom to love, even as God loves. Love is what happens when freedom reigns. If we should ask what is the freedom which grace gives, we should have to answer: It is the freedom to love, to be like God. In the last analysis, it is love and not logic that will construct the most eloquent response to atheism in our time. It is a love always at work on the vast frontiers of freedom, always on the lookout to challenge new forms of oppression and slavery.

NOTES

1. Benedetto Croce, *History as the Story of Liberty* (New York, 1955), p. 57.

2. *Ibid.*, p. 57.

3. Cf. Langdon Gilkey, *Naming the Whirlwind: The Renewal of God-Language* (Indianapolis: Bobbs-Merrill, 1969), esp. pp. 365-397.

4. Cf. Wolfhart Pannenberg, "Reden von Gott angesichts atheisticher Kritik," *Evangelischer Kommentare* (August, 1969), pp. 442-446.

5. Whether fact or fiction, there is a story about Napoleon Bonaparte claiming that the existence of the Jews is his reason for believing in God.

6. Wolfhart Pannenberg, *Theology and the Kingdom of God* (Philadelphia: Westminster Press, 1969), p. 63.

7. *The Lutheran* (December 17, 1969), p. 30.

8. Ernst Käsemann, *Jesus Means Freedom* (Philadelphia: Fortress Press, 1969).

9. *Ibid.*, p. 17.

10. *Ibid.*

11. *Ibid.*, p. 59.

12. *Ibid.*, p. 85.

13. Jean Paul was the popular name of the poet, Johann Paul Friedrich Richter (1763-1825).

14. Martin Luther, *The Large Catechism, Book of Concord*, ed. by Theodore Tappert (Philadelphia: Fortress Press, 1959), p. 365.

15. For a similar line of argument, see Traugott Koch, "Gott—der Grund der Freiheit," *Pastoral Theologie*, Vol. 57 (1968), pp. 45ff.

16. Cf. Jürgen Moltmann, "The Revolution of Freedom: Christians and Marxists Struggle for Freedom," *Religion, Revolution and the Future*, trans. by M. Douglas Meeks (New York: Charles Scribner's Sons, 1969).

17. Cf. Theodore Roszak, *The Making of a Counter Culture* (Garden City: Doubleday & Company, 1969).

18. Nicholas Berdyaev, *Slavery and Freedom* (New York: Charles Scribner's Sons, 1944), p. 89.

19. On the different ways of conceiving transcendence, see J. Moltmann's "The Future as New Paradigm of Transcendence," *Religion, Revolution and the Future*, pp. 177-199.

# 3

# Resurrection
# Hope and Personal
# Identity

Immanuel Kant is remembered for many pithy statements. One that every beginning student of philosophy learns is: "Concepts without percepts are empty; percepts without concepts are blind." The wisdom of this dialectical realism can be applied to the resurrection of Jesus. There are some theologians who, doubtful of the possibility of verifying the resurrection as a historical *fact,* would wish nonetheless to talk about its *meaning.* Relinquishing the fact of the resurrection, they will cling resolutely to its meaning. The question, however, cannot be easily dismissed—whether meanings without facts are not empty—especially in a religion that stands or falls with its historical character. In Christianity the spirit is not without flesh, the soul is not without body. Gnosticism or docetism are still the enemies of a historical faith.

On the other hand, there are some theologians who argue vehemently for the facticity of the resurrection. But what can they say about its meaning? It is possible to hold the line on the resurrection as part and parcel of the entire controversy about the Bible. The Bible is an inspired book of true assertions, and the resurrection is one of them. Or perhaps one defends the resurrection as part of the Christian tradition, as one of the phrases in the Apostles' Creed. Holding to the resurrection as fact for the sake of the Bible and the Creed does nothing to make it meaningful as an expression of faith. To place belief in the resurrection purely on the basis of

authority militates against the effort to make it mean something valid in terms of modern anthropology, in terms of
man's self-understanding today. The question to ask is
whether facts without meanings are not blind, especially in a
religion that is mission to every present, that seeks to proclaim its truth to all men, at all times, in all places, that offers
life and salvation under the conditions of every class, culture,
and language. If the resurrection is the eschatological event
with universal validity, as it is within the horizon of primitive
Christianity, then its meaning must be brought to expression
under the most varied conditions of man's quest for personal
identity and fulfillment.

## THE UNDERDEVELOPED THEOLOGY OF RESURRECTION

In his most recent essay on the resurrection,[1] Wolfhart
Pannenberg provides a survey in which he shows how both
in the history of Christian thought and in contemporary
systematic theology the resurrection is a vastly underdeveloped part of Christian theology. Underdevelopment means a
number of things:

First, it means that with few possible exceptions (e.g.,
Walter Künneth[2]) the theme of the resurrection in modern
Christologies lags far behind its position in primitive Christianity. Treatments of the resurrection have not caught up
with the results of modern critical historical research. This
research acknowledges that the resurrection of Jesus is the
basis of the apostolic proclamation of the salvation of mankind. In all probability the christological titles and utterances
are applied to Jesus on the basis of the Easter event. Without
the resurrection belief there would hardly have been a sufficient motive to go on preaching the story of Jesus as the
medium of salvation.

Second, theology of the resurrection is nearly eclipsed by
theology of the cross in Western theology, in marked contrast to the Eastern church. In the West, both in Roman
Catholicism before and after the Council of Trent and in

Reformation theology, the main stress was on the atoning death of Jesus on Calvary. Salvation was preached and accepted chiefly in terms of reconciliation from guilt and atonement for sin, effected by the vicarious sufferings and death of Christ. As Gustaf Aulén argues so well in *Christus Victor,* this Western theology of the death of Jesus as a sacrifice or satisfaction gives a complete account of salvation without any essential connection with the resurrection. Not that the resurrection was denied, but it tended to be a sequel to the story of salvation.

Third, the breakup of Protestant orthodoxy brought about the beginning of a new christological development. The impact of the Enlightenment was such, however, that Christology did not move ahead to incorporate the resurrection as foundationally important; rather, it recurred to the earthly life of Jesus. Christology was presented as the religion of Jesus or his exemplary moral teachings and life-style. Liberal Christologies gave up the authority of the Bible, but placed great weight on the authority of Jesus. Paul Tillich spoke of these liberal Christologies as Jesuologies, because they present Christology in the form of a life of Jesus. The soteriological focus is directed away from the cross and resurrection of Jesus.

Fourth, the recurrence to the life of the historical Jesus was not an exclusively liberal preoccupation. The conservatives also produced biographies of Jesus as one immediately transparent to God. Beginning with the virgin birth they interpreted the life of Jesus as a demonstration of the fact of the incarnation. Hence the miracles of Jesus proved that he was divine, and his predictions that he shared the omniscience of God. The liberals, on the other hand, dispensed with the dogmas bracketing the life of Jesus, that is, the dogmas of incarnation and atonement interpreting the birth and death of Jesus. Instead, they wanted only the inner life or religious consciousness of the mature man Jesus. They believed they witnessed in his own religious life a high revelation of God; the teachings and activities of Jesus are expressions of a magnetic spirituality, drawing others into his orbit of influence.

Faith in Jesus is imitation of his life. In no way does the resurrection play an important role in the liberal "lives of Jesus."

Fifth, the underdeveloped character of the resurrection as an integral doctrine of the faith cannot be laid to the Western church alone. It happened much earlier in the ancient church, going back to what Adolf von Harnack called the Hellenization of Christianity. On Hellenistic soil the preaching of the earliest Christian kerygma underwent a shift of focus from the resurrection to the incarnation. Instead of the incarnation being posited on the basis of the resurrection, as a kind of legendary prologue to the revelation of God in the crucified and risen Jesus, now the resurrection becomes interpreted as but a natural outcome of the incarnation of the eternal Son of God. On Hellenistic soil the events in the ministry of Jesus are interpreted *forward* as illustrations of the incarnation, instead of *backward* from the light of Easter and Pentecost. Who is Jesus of Nazareth? He is the Son of God walking around on earth for awhile. That would have been an impossible combination of concepts on Jewish ground. But it was a brilliant adjustment of the gospel to the missionary situation. Today we would call it "indigenization." Yet the price was high. The thought occurred that if Jesus is filled with the imperishable life of the immortal God, then he did not really suffer and die. He was faking these things, making it appear that he was limited by finitude as all other mortals. This is the meaning of "docetism," a word that derives from the Greek *dokein*, meaning "to seem, to appear." Hence the resurrection is a case of the grave not being able to contain one who is essentially immortal. The resurrection is more like pulling back the curtain to reveal who was there on the stage all along.

Another aspect of the problem of interpreting Jesus forward from the dogma of the incarnation is that it gives rise to innumerable exegetical *tours de force*. The dogmatic exegete struggles with the question: "How could Jesus do this or that if he is really God?" The temptations of Jesus were all mishandled because the Gospel accounts were at odds with the aprioristic reasoning from the dogma of the incarnation. Even after the Council of Chalcedon, which was a victory for the Nestorian stress on the real humanity of Jesus, orthodox Christology in both East and West never really shed its docetic leanings. Orthodoxy finds it difficult to affirm the real humanity of Jesus, that he was a human being subject to the relativities of existence in history.

The question today is whether Christology can be given a new beginning. I believe it can, indeed, that it already has. Wolfhart Pannenberg's major theological book is such a Christology, *Jesus—God and Man*.³ It proceeds from a fundamental recognition of the importance of the resurrection within the structure of primitive Christian faith; it integrates modern historical critical findings into our contemporary confession of who Jesus is and what he means for us today; it also takes seriously the correlation of the resurrection to the self-understanding of man. This last is an important dimension of the theological problem of the resurrection, for granted that we may acknowledge its importance to the first Christians, why should we as latter-day Christians believe it, especially if it calls for a sacrifice of the intellect?

## PROBLEMS FOR A THEOLOGY OF THE RESURRECTION

A new Christology which orients itself around the confession of the risen Jesus has to contend with many difficult problems:

First, the one problem that springs to the mind faster than any other has to do with the historicity of the resurrection. Even Jürgen Moltmann, who places his whole theology of hope on the resurrection, concedes that "we cannot verify the event itself."⁴ He feels compelled to admit that "the act of the raising of Jesus is not a historically observable and ascertainable event."⁵ Another example: Gerald O'Collins can claim, on the one hand, that Christian hope is radically determined by the resurrection of the crucified Jesus and, on the other hand, admit that "the resurrection of Christ is not appropriately described as 'historical.' Historians deal with events that are localizable in space and datable in time. The resurrection is not an event *in* space and time."[6] The problem is how to speak of events that by definition stand outside space and time. At least some of the followers of the theology of hope, especially those heavily influenced by the early Barth and Bultmann, wish to place great stress on the resurrection and at the same time place it in limbo beyond history. This achieves the result of withdrawing it from historical investigation and of making it an assertion of faith that stands on its own footing. There is real disagreement within the campgrounds of the eschatological theologians. We could not say that Pannenberg and Moltmann agree. Moltmann thinks that Pannenberg is trying to prove the resurrection by historical arguments. Pannenberg fears that faith becomes arbitrary and self-deluding if its contents are relegated to an "invulnerable area" in which no rational methods of verification can be applied. Perhaps there is a middle way between those who try to prove too much and those who wish to verify nothing at all.

Second, it must be admitted that there are risks connected with any method of treating the resurrection of Jesus. Perhaps we can say that we ought to permit every assertion of faith to be tested as far as possible by critical historical procedures. This way we minimize the risk of obscurantism, of a superstitious clinging to myths and legends that cannot face any truth tests, or holding to beliefs for which there are no reasonable grounds. I recall a useful distinction once made by John Macquarrie: it is reasonable, though it is not rational.[7] If the resurrection happened at all or if something about it was observed to have happened in our world, within the horizon of our historical experience, and was made the subject of historical witnesses and reports, then we cannot place the resurrection in a historical DMZ. I believe that we must agree fully with Pannenberg on this score. The resurrection cannot be placed off-limits to historical inquiry. This means that we accept Pannenberg's method of handling certain common objections to the resurrection.

Third, one of these objections stems from an empiricoscientific prejudice. It actually goes back to David Hume, who said that any assertion that a dead man has been raised is to be disclaimed from the beginning, because it would contradict all analogies from our experience. The very uniqueness of the resurrection is sufficient reason to dismiss it, since we cannot have knowledge of things which exist or occur without analogy. It has also been said that natural science cannot tolerate the idea of a dead person coming back to life again. In face of these objections we have to maintain that every historical event is unique, that insofar as something really new ever happens, there is an element within it that is unlike every other. Every contingent historical event is in one sense "without analogy." This means there is something nonrecurrent and nonreducible in every truly historical event, otherwise history would be like nature; it would not be moving forward to the future of anything new. We could even ask whether nature does not also have a history, whether the view of nature as moving cyclically in a closed system is not an optical illusion. It would be pointless to enter into a conflict with the natural sciences on the resurrection. That would arise from a misunderstanding from both theologians and scientists. It is the function of natural science to describe regular patterns and recurrent structures in the process of nature. That is the essence of its success story. Conflict with natural science would arise only if the resurrection would mean a suspension of the so-called laws of nature, so that the scientist would be compelled to cease being a scientist. But that is not the case, since the laws function in the natural world all the way to death. Whether there is another kind of story to tell is not within the purview of the natural sciences.

Fourth, there is a theological problem to be considered. For Christians of the pietist, anti-intellectualist bent every historical examination of the records is irrelevant. Why? Because the resurrection is the initial event of a new world of God; it cannot be perceived by the eyes of the old world which function only under the conditions of ordinary knowledge. The trouble with this position is that if it were carried to its logical conclusion it would react against every assertion of God's presence and activity in the ordinary world. Nothing of God's work in history could be narrated. We would be afflicted by a brutal dualism in which the world of the new can never penetrate the world of the old. This is apocalypticism with a gnostic twist, a form of it that we reject totally. The genuine Christian affirmation is that the realm of the new breaks into the old, so that we see with our eyes and hear with our ears what the Spirit is trying to communicate to those who are loved by God for Christ's sake.

Fifth, the accounts of the resurrection are not all of equal value or significance. The reports of the empty tomb do not count as much as the reports of the witnesses who encountered Jesus as a living person after his crucifixion. The *Urdatum* of resurrection faith is the conviction that Jesus is no longer dead but alive. Should that be called a historical event? By such a question we are asking whether it happened in a definite place. We have to answer, "Yes, in Jerusalem— or at least in Palestine." Did it happen at a definite time? Again we have to answer, "Yes, a short time after his death, and certainly before the apostles dispersed to preach the gospel of a crucified Jew." At least from the standpoint of those who issued the first reports, the resurrection happened at a definite time and place. Does that warrant calling it a historical event? From another standpoint, no. For all other historical events in time and space are linked up with the effects they produce in an interlocking way on the same plane of observable phenomena. But if Jesus was raised from the dead, this is not one event in an interconnected series on the same level; it is a new beginning. It puts an end to one series of events heading toward death, and begins a quite new order of life that dies no more. The new life into which Jesus advanced is beyond our range of perception. The witnesses in space and time testified to a reality that transcends the conditions of existence. "He is risen" means that Jesus is liberated from the conditions of finitude and is therefore united with the source of freedom in the absolute future. This freedom can be exercised also to make possible his real presence in, with, and under the material signs in the sacramental experience. It is this dual character of the resurrection reality—freedom from and freedom for—which accounts for the fact that some theologians are willing, others are unwilling, to call the resurrection a historical event. If one looks to the reception of the event, namely, to the witnesses who passed on the reports of what they heard and saw, we would call the resurrection a historical event. If one looks, on the other hand, to the nature of the reality that appeared to the witnesses, then we might well hesitate to call the resurrection a historical fact. Those who call it a historical event have to reckon with the fact that he who appeared as alive again after his death has now disappeared and is no longer available as an object of sensory perception. Those who do not call it a historical event have to reckon with the fact that the event the Gospels report occurred within a historical framework; it could be the object of historical reporting and remembering.

I am inclined to think that this apparent dissensus among those who believe in the real presence of the risen Christ is due to an inner structure of the event itself. It is not due to deficient reason, lack of faith, bad will, or some such thing. The reason is objective, not subjective. It is objective in the sense that the resurrection as an event within the horizon of history is at the same time an eschatological event. The eschatological incursion breaks open the historical frame and sets it in motion in a self-transcending way. History overshoots itself when it becomes the matter of eschatological creativity. Therefore I would say that the resurrection is at least a historical event, else it would probably not have survived the death of the myths of the dying and rising gods. But it is more than a historical event, or it would not be the ground of hope and the inexhaustible source of courage to face the future in hope, in spite of our having to die. With this statement we turn to the meaning of the resurrection as an eschatological event. It is an event with existential meaning; it bears on the ultimate question of life, to be or not to be, to live or not to live, to look forward to nullification or transfiguration.

## The Resurrection as the Eschatological Event

As an eschatological event the resurrection is not the mere terminal point of Jesus' life; it is the new beginning beyond the last negation of life. The resurrection is the death of the last enemy; it is the power to overcome the deadliness of death itself. This event was not so much that the incarnation of eternal life had survived death, but that the eschatological future of life had entered the realm of the dying and had conquered it inside its stronghold.

We do not know the exact nature of the resurrection event. But we cannot let go the assertion that something really happened. The most appropriate way to speak of Jesus is as one presently alive, now the leading participant in the drama of life beyond the history of death. If we cannot *in fact* verify the resurrection as a historical event, we can nevertheless affirm that *in principle* it is verifiable. We are making an assertion that we count as true, and therefore something that we acknowledge to be knowable. To appropriate a concept of John Hick, it is subject to "eschatological verification."[8] The verification is something yet to occur and therefore now to be anticipated. It shall be known for what it really is from an end-historical perspective, that is, when history can be seen from the standpoint of its end, when the whole of history can be known, holiscopically and not only fragmentarily. Under the conditions of finite historical existence, the proof is provisional, existential, a life-wager, still open to the future, and not something that can be registered and assigned to the graveyard of inertial facts. The resurrection is that kind of fact that, in addressing us with its power, throws us in expectation forward upon the future. It is that kind of fact that makes a new future. If one has a low regard for facts, as just so many dead items lying frozen in the past, or as mere ciphers in a history book, one will not wish to call the resurrection a fact. But if a fact receives its meaning in the open process of history, that is, from its future, then the resurrection can be called a fact; it is the beginning of a qualitatively new history.

The resurrection as an event is not only a basis of hope for

the future; it is the power of the future becoming present
now; it is the place where eschatology and history become
fully identical. The resurrection not only points to the future;
it is the future entering the present. The future of fulfillment
that is anticipated is also embodied in Jesus. This embodiment is traced back to the beginning of Jesus' life—his birth.
In this way the doctrine of the incarnation is established.
The future of God achieved its unique enfleshment in Jesus,
from the beginning of his finite existence. The resurrection
as an eschatological event means that it is not a mere historical datum, to be taken under our cognitive control; it is
an event with power to change things, to direct history toward
its ultimate aim. Its meaning is opened up to us only in the
process of our conversion. Only those who confess Jesus as
Lord of their lives actually confess that he is risen from the
dead.

What if the resurrection is an answer to a question no one
is asking? One reads on backhouse walls: "There will be no
Easter this year; they've found the body." So what would
change? Is the resurrection a liberating word in history? Is it
good news to modern man? Does it answer to the modern
question of fragmentariness, or of absurdity? If a person
cannot hope for fulfillment beyond death, is there something
else that can grant the sense of fulfillment? Is there anything
to which a man can give his life, some cause for which he
can spend it, that is not itself among the ambiguities of life?
These are difficult questions. We will present only one line
that may be worth pursuing.

The main reason for demythologizing and for existential
interpretation is to make sense out of the Easter story to ourselves as modern men. I have never doubted that interpretation is needed, that every preacher worth his salt must do a
lot of demythologizing—or perhaps remythologizing. Especially because this is so, it is important that we be guided by
a sound sense of the human question to which the message
of the resurrection can provide an answer. If, as you see on
the billboards, Jesus is the answer, what is the question?

People are asking today for a transcendent meaning of life,

something more than the source of the questionable values of culture and morality in their concrete historical forms. A person looks for a fulfilling future which brings his life to a meaningful outcome, to ground a sense that he has not lived for nought. To offer a man the possibility of fulfilling his life by offering it up to society, by sacrificing himself to his nation, or for the future development of the race, or for the glory of his tribe and group—all that is not met with enthusiasm. It seems hollow—none of that is equal to a human life. On the one hand, we are living in a time when people are affirming the secular world, but if we rightly hear the prophets of the counter-culture, there is less and less in the glorious secular vision of technological man to allay the pangs of finitude. The message of the appearance of true life and new being in the resurrection of Jesus as the victory over death, innocent suffering, and broken existence may offer a ground of hope that overshoots the very questionable and fragmentary structures of secular society. Man as man is afflicted by a hunger for love, healing, freedom, and righteousness that cannot be satisfied by any of the structures with which he is allied in the present time. Man has a passion to be wholly human that cannot be satisfied by the roles he plays and the houses and cars he owns or by the success he gains in his upward strivings. When he races into the future or turns the clock ahead, he is only shortening the distance between now and his time for dying.

The question to which the resurrection may provide an answer is the question of an adequate definition of man. Can man be adequately defined in his humanness if a boundary line is fixed beyond which he cannot seek his identity in fulfillment and pure freedom? Is not man a creature in quest of a total unburdening, a full freedom, in which all the negativities are themselves negated? Can man have his future closed for him, closed absolutely and with utter finality by death? Will he not rather create a myth to enshrine a vision beyond the closure? And is that myth to be classified merely as wishful thinking? Or, if it is wishful thinking, can we not learn something true about man from the fact that he dreams and wishes and fantasizes beyond the present limits of finitude?

I have stated that the resurrection is an answer to the question of man's more adequate self-definition. That is a question of the future of man's identity. In the New Testament we hear less about the immortality of the soul than about the resurrection of the body. I would like to believe that there is a significant meaning in this distinction. Inasmuch as the resurrection hope includes the body, we do not find the meaning of our identity by fleeing the body and bodily relationships. I cannot be without my body. Even in a dream it is impossible to struggle free of the body and maintain the sense of personal identity. The hope for the eschatological future of God is not a flight from the body into a cool place where souls exist in a dreamy vaporlike state. It is a hope which releases the power of the future, which we have traditionally called eternal life, into the body of this life, into the personal, social, and political body of this life.

In modern culture, those raising the question of personal meaning and identity in the most earnest way often find in drugs or transcendental meditation a means of escape. I call it a means of escape, of copping out, because they leave the body behind; they leave the field of battle in which they have experienced an infinite boredom. Since life in the body and in bodily relationships seems boring, futureless and meaningless, they find a way to freak out, to unite themselves with what Theodore Roszak calls a "Counterfeit Infinity."[9] The LSD kick is a trip into a timeless paradise. I saw a graffito saying: "Drugs are the opiate of the people." They are the new means to immortality of the soul, apart from the beautiful body.

This quest for personal salvation outside the body of the individual and of society is not the way of resurrection hope. Resurrection hope looks to a future which is steadily seeking to incorporate our bodily present, which persistently seeks to enflesh itself in social and political ways. The resurrection hope makes it possible to live more fully in the present, because one does not demand from the present or any of its institutions the ultimate fulfillment. One can dare to throw oneself into the present with abandon and to be truly open without clutching and to be free only if one's future is secured in hope. A man will find himself in the kingdom of God if he is part of its coming in the present, if he takes up his cross. The future of the resurrection can be mirrored back into the present through the power of love, which can create new life and pursue the works of freedom. Love is the power to free us up.

Resurrection hope derives its ethic from the eschatological principle of life which Jesus enunciated: "For whoever would save his life will lose it; and whoever loses his life for my sake and the gospel's will save it" (Mark 8:35). A man can find his identity in this life only if he reaches beyond to the ultimate future of life, of unity and wholeness, of peace and fullness, of love and righteousness. He can reach beyond, because the eschatological future of life to which he reaches has arrived already in the resurrection of Jesus. In this way, and for this reason, the New Testament calls Jesus Christ the Ground of Hope—the Risen Lord.

### NOTES

1. Wolfhart Pannenberg, "Dogmatische Erwägungen zur Auferstehung Jesu," *Kerygma und Dogma,* 14 (1968), 105–18.

2. Walter Künneth, *The Theology of the Resurrection* (St. Louis, Mo.: Concordia Publishing House, 1965).

3. Philadelphia: Westminster Press, 1968.

4. Jürgen Moltmann, *Religion, Revolution and the Future* (New York: Charles Scribner's Sons, 1969), p. 50.

5. *Ibid.*

6. Gerald O'Collins, *Man and His New Hopes* (New York: Herder and Herder, 1969), p. 69.

7. Cf. John Macquarrie's discussion on reason in *Principles of Christian Theology* (New York: Charles Scribner's Sons, 1966), pp. 15ff.

8. John Hick, "Religious Statements as Factually Significant," *The Existence of God,* ed. by John Hick (New York: Macmillan Company, 1964), pp. 259ff.

9. Theodore Roszak, *The Making of a Counter Culture* (Garden City: Doubleday & Company, 1969), p. 155.

# 4

# Eschatology and Ontology in Conflict: A Study of Paul Tillich's Theology

Paul Tillich struggled with the problem of eschatology from the beginning of his career to the end. In the early 1920s, as the theological leader among the religious socialists, he fought to recover the prophetic foundations of modern socialism. The task was to overcome the latter's immanentalist utopianism by means of a transcendentalist eschatology. In the 1960s Tillich was completing the last part of his *Systematic Theology* on "History and the Kingdom of God." He let the problem of eschatology arise as the question of the meaning and goal of history, and therefore as the "quest for the kingdom of God." His answer was given, however, in terms of a kingdom-of-God eschatology whose fundamental frame of reference was an essentialist ontology. The result? The problem of the future was solved by throwing it outside the more limited (in Tillich's system) framework of a historical eschatology into that of a transhistorical ontology. The future end of history was elevated into the permanent presence of eternal life. This process of being elevated through participation in eternal life in the existential now is called "essentialization."[1] Essentialization is the return of existence to essence from whence it originated, not a mere return to the emptiness of being at the beginning, but a return, nevertheless, to original being, presumably now richer and fuller for having passed through historical exis-

54

tence. The doctrine of essentialization, in the last analysis, means the translation of the eschatological future into the mystical presence of being itself. Theological eschatology becomes a little wheel within the big wheel of a theological ontology. Eschatology becomes demythologized, not by the force of some modern idiom, but by that tried and tested but rarely true assistant in the clarification of the Christian message—Platonic mystical ontology. Tillich states: "Eschatology deals with the relation of the temporal to the eternal."[2] This could just as well be given as the definition of the ontology of Plato or Plotinus. What is lacking in this definition to make it useful as a theological definition of eschatology is the specificity of history's irreversible movement toward the future.

## Two Types of Categories

The elevation of biblical eschatology into Platonizing essentialism did not occur without signals of great stress in Tillich's thought. In fact, on close inspection the tensions become so glaring that one may speak of an unresolved contradiction between Tillich I and Tillich II. This risky assertion must, however, immediately be cleared of possible misunderstandings. We are not saying that there are two Tillichs in a chronological sense, as if the contradiction lies between the earlier European and the later American periods of his career. Rather, the contradiction lies between two sides, two sources, two types of thinking, two sets of categories, which coexisted in his mind from the beginning to the end. Tillich was aware of this contradiction, but he preferred to view it as a contrast. The two sides of the contrast can and must be maintained in a system of mediation, by the method of correlation. Of what does this contradiction, or this contrast, consist? It consists of "the struggle between time and space,"[3] to use the title of one of Tillich's essays. It consists of the tension between a spatialistic ontology and a temporalistic eschatology, between the predominance of the past and the priority of the future, between the motion of the circle and the flight of the arrow, between the horizontal expectation of the kingdom of God and the vertical leap into eternal life, between a transcendence shining through as a dimension of depth in the present and a transcendence breaking in as the future from ahead. Tillich was aware of the struggle; he was equally aware that it would be resolved in any one system of thought always to the advantage of one side or the other. With enviable clarity he compared two types of interpretation of history, the historical and the nonhistorical.[4] In the nonhistorical type, history is interpreted through nature; in the historical type, history is interpreted through history. In the one, space is predominant; in the other, time. "Religion as well as philosophy must choose between these two possibilities *which ultimately are exclusive. And this choice is the decision against or for Christianity.*"[5]

One further qualification of this contrast between Tillich I and Tillich II must be added. In spite of our assertion that the contrasting sides in Tillich's theology do not correspond to an earlier and a later stage of his developing thought, it is demonstrably true that the existential-ontological side of this thinking was most visibly projected in America, whereas the historical-eschatological side was worked out in his earlier religio-socialist writings in Germany, most of which remain untranslated and unknown to his American critics. We could hazard the reason for this. The creative use of historical-eschatological categories presupposed intimate familiarity with the concrete socio-political situation. Categories from prophetic and apocalyptic eschatology, such as *kairos,* the demonic, the kingdom of God, could be used in critical and constructive ways only within the situation in which the prophet himself stood, and which he therefore *understood.* When the scene shifted to America, Tillich was in a state of personal disappointment. The *kairos* of a new theonomy, of a new society transparent to its religious ground, reaching new measures of personal depth, economic justice, social equality, political freedom, did not materialize. Instead the demons of national socialism rushed in to fill the space. The social and political situation in America was unfamiliar to Tillich. That side of his theology which pre-supposed the "proletarian situation"[6] became inactive; only random *ad hoc* and often half-hearted utterances vis-à-vis the social-economic-political situation in America and the world were made by Tillich during his American period. One needs only to compare these bland utterances to the imagina-tive, pioneering articles and books Tillich wrote earlier on the Christian roots of socialism and the task of theology and the church in relation to the further development of social-ism in a mass, technological culture. If the change in context threw Tillich's theology out of focus, socially speaking, he could still presuppose that the individual man and his needs were quite similar in Europe and America. The image of the alienated individual that emerged in Europe between the wars finally surfaced in America twenty years later, when college students read existentialist literature and studied depth psychology. The after-effects of the depression and two world wars, which brought grist to the mills of existentialism in Europe, began to be felt in America as well. On university campuses and among disillusioned intellectuals Tillich could fascinate an audience with his existentialist diagnosis and his gutturally mystical answers spoken so sincerely *de profundis*. This was the voice of Tillich II. It did not do justice to the element of expectation, of hope, in the Christian faith and to the irreducible futurity of the future in theological escha-tology, which Tillich went to some lengths to articulate when he dealt with the distinctively Christian and biblical idea of the kingdom of God.

We will now delineate some of the features of Tillich's eschatological interpretation of history, which we believe stand, not merely in contrast, but in contradiction to his essentialist ontology. Then we will show how these features are eroded away by ontological categories in the interest of overcoming the antinomies of strictly historical thinking.

The end result is that Tillich's assimilation of the historical thinking of socialism into the prophetic eschatology of the Bible failed because both were betrayed into the hands of a suprahistorical ontology that came from Neoplatonic mysticism.

"Christianity is essentially historical."[7] History is a movement in which the new is created, in which unique and unrepeatable events occur, and which runs toward a future goal. "Biblical religion is eschatological."[8] That means, Christianity looks ahead toward a future transformation of reality, interprets the past and acts in the present in light of that future, the goal toward which history runs.[9] In Christianity, unlike Buddhism and Greek philosophy, "the New Being is expected predominantly in a horizontal direction rather than a vertical one."[10] Redemption takes place *in* and *through* history, not by climbing a ladder of perfection into eternity above history. In the Christian prophetic view, there is not a mystical longing for fusion into the Eternal One. There is expectant hoping for the realization of the kingdom of God, the divine rule of universal peace, love, and righteousness in a new heaven and a new earth.[11]

In its encounter with gnosticism in the ancient period and with Nazism in modern times, Christianity was saved by the Old Testament from the loss of its historical rootedness and its Abraham-like trust in the God of time, the God of history. Abraham was called "to follow the God of time and the future who is the God of all nations."[12] Abraham struck out into the future, leaving his homeland and the gods of the hearth, "of soil and blood, of family tribe and nation; that is, the gods of space, the gods of paganism and polytheism, the gods who stand beside each other."[13] This is no commentary on an ancient legend, it is a polemic against the neopaganism of the "German Christians." Christianity, following the Old Testament, broke with the "myth of origin" which presents history in terms of rotation and recurrence, in terms of cyclical revolution or periodical return.[14] Christianity is not controlled by the myth of origin. Where this myth prevails, there is no room for anything really new in history; time falls under the predominance of space. The past holds the present in bondage to the whence of origins. The criterion of what is right or good or true now is whether it recapitulates the past, whether it reverts back to beginnings. Tillich fought against this tendency that was and is so much alive in the church and society. In a revealing admission he once wrote, "Ontology stands on the basis of the myth of origin, and is bound to space. Ontology must also make time into something spatial. It is the final and most abstract version of the myth of origin."[15] Then he adds that ontology can retain its validity only when it is broken open by philosophy of history. A "fundamental ontology" which is not conceived historically must be avoided.[16]

There can be no doubt that Tillich saw the danger of fitting eschatology into ontology, time into space, history into nature. The question is whether he did not tip the scale against history and against its eschatological future with his idea of essentialization. The new being is preset by an ontology of being as such, and therefore the vision of the eschatological end looks too much like the ontologized myth of origin. From another aspect, the question is whether the category of expectation in the Christian faith is given its due. In his book, *The Socialistic Decision,* one can see promising beginnings toward a "theology of hope." Instead of "hope" Tillich uses the word "expectation." The attitude of expectation presses toward a promised future. The element of expectation, so pronounced in socialism, betrays its genetic connection with biblical prophetism. "Nobody can understand socialism if he overlooks its prophetic character."[17] Expectation is the prophetic principle and the principle of socialism. It is a state of tension toward the future, since it is oriented to something that does not exist, but ought to, something that has never been, but one day will be. Since the new that is expected is essentially historical, the attitude to the present must be critical. If the new were suprahistorical, one could remain indifferent to the present and seek salvation through withdrawal and self-elevation. Expectation would not trigger off the will to change things in the present if it were solely for the soul and its flight to the eternal. Hope became otherworldly and individualized in orthodoxy and pietism. Tillich detected the same fatal error in the neo-Lutheran political theology of Friedrich Gogarten, whose version of the two-kingdom doctrine offered an ideological defense for the "powers that be."[18] Expectation lives for history, but it lives from the future. In Christian faith it is down-to-earth, not a leap into another world; it prays for the coming of God's kingdom, not for an escape from the prison of reality. Does Tillich's idea of essentialization do justice to the future-directedness of expectation, or does it not dissolve expectation into a passive sinking into the depths of the present through which the eternal shines? Does not mysticism finally pull the nerve out of hope? If this is the case, as I think it is, then it is not proper to speak of a balance in tension between two poles of thinking. Rather, one must reckon with a contradiction between irreconcilable opposites, held together not by an intrinsic dialectic, but by a formidable theological will power.

## FROM HISTORY TO MYSTICISM

Here we can trace only briefly how it happened that Tillich's thinking slipped from historical eschatology into mystical ontology.

*A. Christ as the Center of History.* Tillich never attained a truly eschatological conception of history. His interpretation of history was christological, but he did not see that eschatology is the prior frame of reference within which the validity of a christological interpretation has to be decided. History can be interpreted as a whole and its meaning can be disclosed only from the end. A christological interpretation is possible and necessary because Christ is the *end of history.* Tillich rarely spoke of Christ as the end of history but, rather, as the center of history. The symbol of the center is ambiguous, however, and quite naturally suggests the image of a circle. It allows one to move, almost without noticing it, from categories of time to categories of space, in relating Christ to history, and God to the world. Tillich was concerned to stress the centrality of Christ, his revelatory and redemptive uniqueness, even the absoluteness of the christological claim in Christianity, and for this purpose he used the symbol, Christ the center of history. On the other hand, he was aware that the biblical claim is that Christ is the end of history. How do these two claims relate to each other? To call Christ the center of history means that the center of gravity lies in the past. On the strength of this symbol Tillich could say, ". . . the center for human consciousness always lies in the past. It cannot be sought in the future, for the meaning of the future is determined by it."[19] The real presence of Christ in the church is thus understood as "the presence of the past in the present."[20] This betrays a noneschatological conception of the reality of Christ in the world today. It does not leave much significance to the future, and to the symbol of Christ as the end of history.

Eschatology joins Christology in the interpretation of history as the doctrine of the ultimate intersecting the center of history from above, revealing the transcendent meaning of history and potentially of every moment of time. In this way the dimension of the future in eschatology could be transvaluated into the self-transcending dimension of every moment of time. Christ as the end of history is thus translated out of the framework of a historical eschatology. He becomes the center of history from which point the irradiating light of eternity reveals depth and meaning.

*B. The Spirit of Utopia.* As a religious socialist Tillich came into contact with the fiery dreams of utopianism. He saw that these dreams were fed by the eschatological projections of the future in Judaism and Christianity. Tillich was a friend of Ernst Bloch, and had positive words to say about Bloch's "Spirit of Utopia" and his "Principle of Hope."[21] No doubt these thoughts stirred in Tillich deep memories of his socialist youth. Several of his later essays dealt with the theme of utopia.[22] In them Tillich reaffirms his lifelong rejection of utopianism, while endorsing the "spirit of utopia."

In affirming the spirit of utopia Tillich was saying that utopia mirrors the inner aim of human existence; that is its *truth*.[23] It reveals what man believes he and his world ought to become. Second, utopia opens up new possibilities anticipated by the imagination; that is its *efficacy*. Today's dreams may become tomorrow's realities. Men without utopias remain stuck to the present; cultures without utopias become stagnant. Third, the spirit of utopia releases courage to change things in the present; that is its *power*. The root of the power is dissatisfaction with the present, aroused and intensified by the gap between the present and the vision of what ought to be.

In spite of going so far with the spirit of utopia, Tillich had to reject utopianism. First of all, utopianism has a false image of man; it slights the seriousness of sin, the depth of alienation. It assumes that the alienation in and between men can be overcome by alienated men. Second, utopianism is fantasy and wishful thinking; it soars beyond what is really possible for men under the conditions of finitude and estrangement. Utopianism becomes inefficacious by blurring the boundaries of what is realistically possible. Third, utopianism leads inevitably to disillusionment, since its hopes are unrealizable. Disillusionment evokes reactions of fanaticism with its terroristic consequences, or of cynicism and apathetic resignation. The common thread running through Tillich's criticisms of utopianism fastens onto its idolatrous attempt to absolutize or infinitize what is merely relative and finite, its attempts to project to ultimate validity what has only penultimacy.

We can follow Tillich both in his justification of the spirit of utopia and in his criticism of utopianism. However, we have to part company with him at the point where he offers a vertical version of mysticism as an alternative to utopianism.

For Tillich the spirit of utopia finds its fulfillment by leaving the horizontal line of expectation altogether, and by getting on a vertical line that ascends above history. The horizontal movement of history toward its fulfillment in the future of God's coming kingdom is pulled into the dialectic between the unconditioned and the conditioned, the eternal and the temporal. The eternal is not a future state of things. It is always present, not only in man (who is aware of it), but also in everything that has being within the whole of being.[24] Traditional dogmatics has always affirmed this, but under a different heading, either as one of the attributes of God (his omnipresence), or under creation and providence. Eschatology in Tillich's doctrine is the epiphany of an eternal presence, or an ecstatic extension of the moment into its own depths where it reaches identity with the eternal. Again, we have to reiterate that this is not the whole of Tillich; it is that side to which we have referred as Tillich II. It is incompatible with Tillich's own statements about history and prophetic hope, and certainly not a fulfillment of the spirit of utopia.

C. *The Kingdom of God and Eternal Life.* The prophetic revolutionary side of Tillich's thought drew its power from the "kingdom of God." He did more than any of the other great theologians of his era to reinstate the "kingdom of God" as a living symbol. The symbol has two sides, an inner-historical and a transhistorical side. When he spelled out the inner-historical meaning of the kingdom of God, he remained within the framework of historical eschatology. The moment he turned to the transhistorical side, to ground history in transcendence, and not abandon it to utopian immanentalism, he applied a conception of the transhistorical, or transcendence, that was launched by Platonic mysticism. At the transhistorical level the symbol of the kingdom of God merges and passes over into the symbol of eternal life. The eschatological image of the end of history is elevated into the permanently present eternal now. The translation of the

symbol of the kingdom of God into eternal life is the door
which lets in the transcendental mysticism that deprives the
mode of future of its meaning.

Tillich was right in laying stress on transcendence. The
question is whether Christianity has to go to Platonic mysticism to get its doctrine of transcendence instead of forging its
own doctrine of transcendence within the horizon of history
and eschatology. It is doubtful that the conceptual difficulties
Tillich felt in handling the idea of the future end of history
can be eased by switching to the space-controlled thinking
of mysticism. In fact, by so doing, real transcendence is not
achieved at all, since it passes over into the immanence of the
eternal now, the permanent present. Transcendence can be
better symbolized by the "future before us," that is, by the
mystery of its power in relation to the past and the present.

*D. The Idea of the* Kairos. The notion that "the divine is
equally near to and equally remote from each period of
history"[25] was once characterized by Tillich as a nonhistorical
conception whose home is Eastern mysticism. I do not think
that Tillich removed himself far enough from this idea. It
influenced his own eschatology. Thus he could say, "the
ultimate stands equally close to and equally distant from
each moment of history."[26] Those are almost identical with
the words quoted above to describe the Asian view of God's
relation to the world. In one of his last essays Tillich lets
himself be carried away into a suprahistorical mysticism in
which the eschatological future has lost all decisive relation
to history. In his essay, "The Decline and the Validity of
the Idea of Progress,"[27] he advances his famous idea of the
*kairos.* The purpose of this doctrine was to steer a middle
way between the pessimism of a transcendental Lutheranism,
which left history to itself, and the optimism of both socialistic utopianism, which thought that society could be totally
changed within history, and progressivistic humanism, which
imagined the world was getting better and better. A *kairos*
is an epochal moment of history in which a new theonomous
society might emerge, not a perfect society but a more perfect

one. This idea of the *kairos*, however, was not sufficiently aligned with the *eschatos*. In this essay, Tillich uses the idea of the *kairos* to assure us that there can be meaningful moments in history, but not a fulfilling future of history. The only fulfillment there is must be snatched now, and the place of its fulfillment is outside time, in eternity. "As a Christian theologian I would say that fulfillment is going on in every moment here and now beyond history, not some time in the future, but here and now above ourselves. . . . Something might happen which is elevated out of time into eternity. This then is a non-Utopian and a true fulfillment of the meaning of history and of our own individual life."[28] History ends in mysticism, and eschatology is elevated into a Platonic heaven.

Our essay on Tillich is not a refutation, but a demonstration and a confession—a demonstration that there are two sides to Tillich, and a confession that we would have placed the accent differently.

## NOTES

1. Paul Tillich, *Systematic Theology* (Chicago: University of Chicago Press, 1963), Vol. III, pp. 400ff.

2. *Ibid.*, p. 298.

3. Paul Tillich, "The Struggle Between Time and Space," *Theology of Culture* (New York: Oxford University Press, 1959), pp. 30ff.

4. Paul Tillich, "Historical and Nonhistorical Interpretations of History: A Comparison," *The Protestant Era* (Chicago: University of Chicago Press, 1948), pp. 16ff.

5. *Ibid.*, p. 17. Italics added.

6. Paul Tillich, "The Protestant Principle and the Proletarian Situation," *The Protestant Era*, pp. 161ff.

7. Paul Tillich, "Historical and Nonhistorical Interpretations of History," *op. cit.,* p. 20.

8. Paul Tillich, *Biblical Religion and the Search for Ultimate Reality* (Chicago: University of Chicago Press, 1955), p. 41.

9. *Ibid.*

10. Paul Tillich, *Systematic Theology*, Vol. II, p. 87.

11. Paul Tillich, "Prophetische und Marxistische Geschıchtsdeutung," *Der Widerstreit von Raum und Zeit, Gesammelte Werke,* Vol. VI (Stuttgart: Evangelisches Verlagswerk, 1963) , pp. 99-100.

12. Paul Tillich, "Historical and Nonhistorical Interpretations of History," *op. cit.,* p. 22.

13. Paul Tillich, "The Struggle Between Time and Space," *op. cit.,* p. 35.

14. Paul Tillich, *Die Sozialistische Entscheidung,* in *Christentum und Soziale Gestaltung, Gesammelte Werke,* Vol. II, p. 237.

15. *Ibid.,* p. 239.

16. *Ibid.*

17. *Ibid.,* p. 310.

18. *Ibid.,* p. 311, n. 3. The particular reference is to Gogarten's writing, *Wider die Achtung der Autorität* (Jena, 1930) and to his *Politische Ethik,* 1932. Then as now, the defense of "law and order" and "respect for authority" can be the rhetorical form the established system uses to conceal its "will to power."

19. Paul Tillich, *The Interpretation of History.* (New York: Charles Scribner's Sons, 1936) , p. 256.

20. *Ibid.,* p. 257.

21. Paul Tillich, "Kairos und Utopie," *Der Widerstreit von Raum und Zeit,* p. 149, and *Systematic Theology,* Vol. III, p. 391. For what Ernst Bloch has to say about Paul Tillich see his recorded statements in *Werk und Wirken Paul Tillichs. Ein Gedenkbuch* (Stuttgart: Evangelisches Verlagswerk, 1967) , pp. 40-41.

22. See "Kairos und Utopie" and "Die Politische Bedeuntung der Utopie im Leben der Völker," in *Der Widerstreit von Raum und Zeit, Gesammelte Werke,* Vol. VI.

23. The following summary is based on "Die Politische Bedeutung der Utopie im Leben der Völker," *op. cit.,* pp. 198ff.

24. Paul Tillich, *Systematic Theology,* Vol. II, p. 400.

25. *Ibid.,* p. 87.

26. Paul Tillich, *The Interpretation of History,* p. 280.

27. Paul Tillich, *The Future of Religions* (New York: Harper & Row, 1966) .

28. *Ibid.,* p. 79.

# 5

# The Rise
# and Fall of Secular
# Christianity

## FACETS OF SECULAR CHRISTIANITY

Slightly over a quarter of a century ago, Dietrich Bonhoeffer uttered the first prophecy in modern times of a totally secular Christianity. We have all been witnesses of the spread of this secular Christianity; I believe we are now seeing it fall. A convenient symbol of the rise and fall of secular Christianity is Harvey Cox's exodus from the "secular city" to the "feast of fools."[1] But as usual, Harvey Cox is not so much the causal agent as the clear symptom of a remarkable shift from a boisterous secular mood to a more religious style of being. There is a new religiosity in the air, perhaps a sign that man cannot live by secular bread alone, but gasps for fresh air of the spirit to create ecstasies of life.

Bonhoeffer's prophecy was that the time was coming soon when there would be no religion at all.[2] The new man of modern times would not be religious any more. He would reach the stage of a radical consciousness without religion. For Christianity this would mean that to survive it would have to become religionless, that is, to discard its outer religious garment with which it has clothed itself for two thousand years. From the very beginning this sounded to some of us like one of the most thrilling absurdities we had ever heard. It was thrilling because we too had experienced religion as an oppression, but still an absurdity because we believed that religion is not merely a law imposed on us from the outside or a passing stage in the evolution of man-

67

kind. Rather, religion arises out of the human condition itself, revealing both a sickness unto death and a longing for lasting life. Religion is a two-dimensional expression, revealing the depth of the human predicament and the struggle for life against death. So when Bonhoeffer prophesied a new man for a "world come of age," in whom there is no concern for "inwardness and conscience" (Bonhoeffer's terms) and no passion for "metaphysics and personal salvation" and no awareness of a need for "God or the church"—we can now say, we have seen such men. The prophecy has come true. We have entered the valley of dry bones (Ezek. 37:1–14) and we have seen skeletons without spirit. We are quite sure the secular model of humanity is a dead-end.

Almost any book you pick up will say that we are living in a secular age. That is what Bonhoeffer saw, so as a Christian with a true instinct he began to ask the missionary question: "How is it possible to be a Christian in a secular epoch?" Do we have to make a man religious before he can become a Christian? Ultimately, Bonhoeffer's concern was a christological one, which I share: how to interpret the Lordship of Christ in a fully secular age. How can the church become free from the fading religious rags of the past and free to embrace the new riches of secular opportunity? Bonhoeffer did not see the secular man as a weakling on his knees eager to receive charity from the church. The secular man is decked out with the virtues of a superman. One must wonder if Bonhoeffer's image of the secular man was not more than a bit influenced by the posters of the ideal Hitler youth. The ideal image of the Hitler youth corresponds in many ways to Bonhoeffer's prophecy of the radically secular man in a world come of age. This link in itself might be enough to arouse suspicion that the outcry of secular Christianity is a false prophecy. It has become a common fallacy in the church that great reverence for the life of the martyr inclines the pious to endow his teachings with prophetic authority, no matter how bizarre. I believe this is the ambiguous fate of Dietrich Bonhoeffer.

There are some obvious aspects of truth in the statement that we are living in a secular time.

First, there is a decline of religious influence in the world. Many traditional symbols, doctrines, and institutions have lost their force. They are ignored or forgotten, and no one is at great pains to refute them any more.

Second, those who still practice a religion are not manifestly different from those who don't. The religious are themselves secularized, since they have turned their attention away from the mysteries, myth, magic, and miracle, and to the things of this world, getting a new kitchen for the church, organizing a bowling team to compete in the church league, a reading group to discuss current fiction, or a sensitivity group so people can find out who they really are.

Third, "we are secular" means that the public realms of government, industry, and education are totally autonomous, and we brook no interference from religion. The elimination of Bible reading from the day's curriculum in school is only a symbol of the divorce between the private and the public. If religion is to exist at all, it must be literally a private matter, kept to one's inner personal life.

Fourth, the secularizing process means that history is not experienced as a field in which divine and antidivine powers are struggling for victory. History is not grounded in God and it has no goal. Man is the measure of what is happening in the world. We proceed as though God did not exist.

Fifth, the world becomes rationalized and desacralized. The experience of the holy in man's communion with nature is transposed into an objectifying attitude, changing nature into material resources, to nourish the insatiable appetites of the machines that technological man has made.

Sixth, the secular society first loses the religion and then the morality that derives from it, so that eventually ends are forgotten for means, values exchanged for facts, endless growth in place of final goals, etc. Man is then created in the image of the machine that he has made, abandoning his self-image as the very image of his Creator. Modern man has gone full circle, rejoining his primitive ancestors in the worship of things he has made with his hands. It was prophesied (Deut. 4:28) that Israel would forget the Lord and "serve gods of wood and stone, the work of men's hands." And there was a curse attached to this prophecy. "Cursed is the man who makes a graven or molten image, a thing made by the hands of the craftsman, and sets it up in secret" (Deut. 27:15). That curse is now upon us, as we live in a system totally dominated by the things of production and consumption.

## THE FALL OF SECULAR THEOLOGY

It was certainly not false for Bonhoeffer to say that we would be living in a secular society. But what is the appropriate Christian response? It could be either of two ways: (1) We could dig ourselves into trenches and ignore the world around us. We could freeze the traditional forms of religion and keep them on ice until the weather gets better outside. We could be defensive, erecting walls around a beleaguered church. We could flee to the desert and set up our own religious enclaves. That is the way of conservatism, of retreat and repristination. (2) Or, we could go the opposite way and welcome all the changes, opening the doors and windows to every wind that blows in from the secular world. We could race our motors to catch up to the modern world, laying aside habits and customs that might identify us as the religious fossils we don't want to be. We want to be fully accepted as modern secular men. Paul van Buren formulates the issue this way: "How can a Christian who is himself a secular man understand his faith in a secular way?"[3] As a follower of Bonhoeffer, that meant *without any religious remainder*. I have found it impossible to be attracted to either way. The conservative way of retreat and retrenchment has always been impossible for me. Its lack of openness to new things and its hardening of the categories are symptoms I was taught to associate with senility. But the modernist way of secular Christianity seemed to me suicidal. To perish by senility or by suicide—that is a question to which I have sought a radically different alternative. As soon as secular Christianity broke upon the scene I wrote these words: "Any church which would try to live by the word of this movement will be writing its own obituary. This Christianity is a cut-flower Christianity, a single generation Christianity."[4]

Those words are even more true to me now in light of the performance principle. How is secular Christianity doing? At first it got all the headlines, proclaiming the death of God. But then it fell into the same grave it had dug for the Divine. The pallor of death fell upon the movement, and its chief sponsors have entered into appropriate silence. However, that does not settle the matter. For in a real sense, the secular Christianity of the left-wing followers of Dietrich Bonhoeffer —John Robinson, William Hamilton, Harvey Cox and Paul van Buren—was not so much a prophecy of a new Christianity to come in the future; rather, these men were unwittingly writing the operative theology of a Christianity that had already become secularized. They were saying, in effect, "We are already secular Christians. What is the theology that fits this situation?" When they said, "God is dead and gone," they were giving expression to a state of affairs they felt to be widespread in Western Christianity. This was the crowning expression of the secularizing process that was reaching into the center of faith itself, long ago announced by Nietzsche and Kierkegaard.

Secular Christianity is not a new phenomenon born in our time. It has been a long time a-coming; its roots go back to the waning of the eschatological consciousness in the church, when it began its accommodation to the Graeco-Roman culture. At the outset I want to lay two suspicions to rest. First, I am not saying that the accommodation could have been avoided. It was the price Christianity had to pay to become a world missionary religion. But for that very reason it would also risk becoming worldly, both *in* the world and *of* the world. Second, I am not saying that accommodation cannot be done successfully. It has been achieved by the great

theologians. What makes them great is the fact that they
were faithful to the truth of the gospel while being free to
express it in radically new terms. The purpose of accommodation is, first, evangelism and then apologetics. False
apologetics is retaining the Christian faith minus its
stumbling-blocks. Secular Christianity represents the de-
scandalization of the gospel.

The waning of the eschatological consciousness means that
the language of God is losing its medium. It is possible to
destroy and remove the conditions of meaningful speech
about God. A Christianity innoculated with the right eschatological serum is immune to secularized religion. God-talk
is kept alive as long as the realm of the future has not
expired into the smug present. If this world is experienced
in its damnation, the question of its possible salvation arises.
It is easy to see why the question of God and the future come
together on the concern for salvation. Belief in God and
belief in the power that will win in the end are one and
the same thing. Without eschatology the figure of God dis-
appears into a hazy mysticism, out of time and out of history.
The Hellenization of the faith effected a mystical dissolution
of the Jewish apocalyptic eschatology, which was the *alma
mater* of the Christian faith. When Yahweh learned Greek,
he stayed home in heaven; when he learned Latin, he turned
the church over to the Roman hierarchy; when he learned
English, he became unemployed and pensioned off. English
empiricism and American pragmatism produced a do-it-
yourself religion, so we close off the theocentric future and
enclose ourselves in the anthropocentric present. This trend
goes back so far and its effects are so widespread that secular
Christianity is only the voice that dares to admit that the
emperor has no clothes.

When God is not the presence who always arrives from the
surprising future, he becomes like an antique, and the church
the museum to house it. To proclaim God without the future
plays into the hands of those who preach the future without
God. Then we get lost in a world becoming more absurd,

rudderless, meaningless, and purposeless. Secular Christianity collapses into the one-dimensionality of the existing world, here-and-now, and has nothing to say when the world becomes more worldly still, that is, when it expires under the burden of its own moment-ridden present without transcendence, without hope for the wholly other reality of the future. Secular Christianity blocks the access of faith to another dimension beyond the present, immersing itself completely into the sole realm of the present and of empirical reality. Perhaps secular Christianity's romance with the present is a reaction to the classical pattern of conservative Christianity, in which the image of God becomes antiquated and God appears to die of old age. But the method of secular Christianity to modernize the old concepts is to hollow them out until they lose their power and appeal. It is just moving with the spirit of the times; it is not really a sufficient counterforce in time to bring new hope to humanity. It places God on such a drastic reducing diet that he becomes too weak to say "no," and his "yes" is only a faint echo of what we have become anyway by "our own reason and strength." Secular Christianity sees no reason to complain because basically it is satisfied with the world as it is, or it believes that nothing is so wrong that man cannot right by his own science and technology.

## THE RISE OF THE NEW RELIGIOSITY

There is no single theological event that has landed a death-blow on secular Christianity. Rather, the significant revolt has come from the secular culture. We are thinking of the rise of the new religiosity and its protest against the impersonal world of facts and data, tools and techniques, degrees and expertise. Thus when secular Christianity cut out religion, as far as the new breed is concerned, it cut out the very heart. So it seems the chickens come home to roost. The result of a Christianity without religion turns out to be not the Christian faith, but the revival of religion without

Christianity. Again we say, man cannot live by the secular alone. There will be outbreakings of religiosity in quest of transcendence. If such enthusiasms are not baptized into faith, they run riot in unbridled emotionalism, irrational mysticism, and self-destructive exoticism.

We look upon the new religiosity as a revelation of the irrelevance of secular Christianity. We must listen to the voices of the new religiosity as an indictment not only of secular society but of the secularized church. I do not see the "death-of-God" theologians as radical or revolutionary at all. Instead, their theology-without-God language was the revealing expression of the bureaucratic do-it-yourself Christianity in which the power of prophetic negation and the presence of spiritual transcendence had already been neutralized. Religiosity lives in all people; it has been suppressed in a culture that functionalizes every human act. Ivan Illich catches the true sentiment of the new religiosity in saying, "I want to celebrate my faith for no purpose at all."[5] It does not have to solve problems, make men better, improve society, clear the slums, end the war, or change the world. The moment that religion is defined *primarily* in categories of social and ethical efficiency, it is dead. The spirit, the ecstasies of holy terror and numinous surprise cannot be rationalized and mechanized. The new religiosity is a desire for mystical experience, for personal participation in meanings and values that transcend secular experience.

Paul Goodman sees the rebellious youth as "a bunch of Luthers in search of a reformation."[6] He sees them in a religious crisis of the magnitude of the Reformation in the 1500s, when not only all institutions but all learning had been corrupted by the whore of Babylon. Modern society and its dominant elites have been operating as if religion were an irrelevant part of the scheme of things, just as the theologians of secular Christianity were saying. The current religious revolt against science and technology stems from a loss of faith in them as instruments that can bring out the glory of man and secure the happiness he seeks. Science and technology are in the hands of greed and power, of those who plan multibillion-dollar budgets to destroy life and wage war on the poor people in the world. Young people are turning away from the secular vision of the future without religion, and instead dabble in magic, astrology, exotic ceremonies, and psychedelic trips. I think this means that the person has come to feel useless in a world dominated by the powers of the corporate state, the military machine, the scientific laboratory and the technocratic apparatus. Religion is the only place with room for useless people. In religion your worth is original, experiential, and immediate. It is not reducible to the function of any institution, because the meaning of the self lies beyond the world. And so people feel alienated in a world that is unequal to the meaning they long for. This feeling of alienation, of estrangement, is a deeply religious experience, but with rare exceptions the church is the last place to which the alienated youth go to commune with a power that transcends the everyday world.

I believe that Theodore Roszak is another commentator who sees the youth revolt as a religious critique of the secular society. He sees the resistance of the counter-culture as a search for a new society which a "human being can identify as home."[7] Home is the place where you feel accepted, just as you are. When home doesn't feel like home, when it too becomes an alienating environment, the children run away. They form a new subculture of the alienated. Roszak compares them to the early Christians in the Roman Empire. They too were estranged from the official culture, fashioning a minority counter-culture out of proletarian types of individuals. The intellectuals of that time ridiculed them as an absurdity. But the apostle Paul accepted the absurdity as a mark in their favor: "For it is written [St. Paul boasted], I will destroy the wisdom of the wise, and will bring to nothing the understanding of the prudent. . . . For the Jews require a sign, and the Greeks seek after wisdom. . . . But God hath chosen the foolish things of the world to confound the wise; and God hath chosen the weak things of the world to con-

found the things which are mighty" (I Cor. 1:19, 22, 27).
Here Paul sounds like some of the far-out spokesmen for the
counter-culture today, heaping contempt on the hallowed
halls of ivy and the politics of the Pentagon. The early Christians were seen as "absolute nobodies, the very scum of the
earth, whose own counter-culture was . . . a few crude symbols, and a desperate longing."[8] Roszak detects an apocalyptic
dimension in the mind of the counter-culture today, com-
parable to the scandalous kerygma of the early church. They
both speak in total terms, total rejection, total catastrophe,
after which will come a totally new way of life, a totally new
future. Of course, there is also a profound difference that we
would be remiss not to mention. It is the difference between
utopianism and eschatology. Utopianism believes optimisti-
cally in the coming of the new after the destruction of the old.
But on what grounds? Eschatology believes in the power of
grace to transform the old in spite of itself—in spite of
decadence and death.

The issue between utopianism and eschatology is that of
the hope of the future. It is the difference between humanism
and Christianity after all. In Christianity there is no way to
go from our collapsing systems to the permanently new
society without invoking the stroke of grace. That is to speak
of God as the power of life against death, as the source of
regeneration, after the first generation of life out of nothing
ends in death. Christianity says, unless we are born again,
we are not born to last. Utopianism gets from the death of
the old to the birth of the new without invoking the power
of grace, without recourse to hope in God as the final counterforce of life against death.

An eloquently naïve example of innocent hope is Charles
Reich's book, *The Greening of America*. Like a messianic
prophet of old, he predicts that a great revolution is coming,
not by violence but by a new consciousness. "Its ultimate
creation will be a new and enduring wholeness and beauty—
a renewed relationship of man to himself, to other men, to
society, to nature, and to the land."[9] Nothing could be more

in keeping with the eschatological hopes in the Bible. When that new creation arrives, truly God's kingdom will have come in all its glory. But the nitty-gritty is this: How will we get from here to there? Reich says the new generation has it already. He sees that the youth of America already possess the new consciousness which will spread like fire to all the people in the land. A conversion of consciousness has already taken place in young people, so that we find there a preliminary sketch or first installment of the brand-new edition of reality that is just around the corner. The new values, the new goals, the new vision, the new freedom, the new consciousness—all these things have already been realized in the new generation of beautiful people under thirty. That is utopianism. Just as Christians believe that their eschatology has achieved its initial realization in the presence of God in Jesus Christ, so this humanism teaches the realization of utopianism here and now in the new generation. The innocence which Christians attribute to their Messiah Jesus is now attributed by Charles Reich to the youth of America. He is compelled to do so, for if he implicated the youth in the same web of sin and guilt, and found them to be driven by the same demons of egoism and hypocrisy as are all too visible in the older generation, he would have no basis for a hope in the future unless he moved his hope onto other foundations. That is a romantic return to Rousseau's noble savage.

Both Theodore Roszak and Charles Reich are utopian humanists who believe that the young are filled with "healthy instincts."[10] Their human nature does not suffer an original perversion, a radical pollution of the self in the depths. They may have a few bad habits, but even some of these they learned from their elders. I don't wish to get into the act of running down the young people. They have enough problems of their own. Twice I have participated in the glorious fun of shutting down our school so that the youthful saviors could get involved in protests and politics to save the world. And both times, except for a few, they frolicked around and

played frisbee. I have seen the new consciousness come up
green in the morning and wither like grass under the noon-
day heat of the sun. The real gap is not the generation gap
between young and old, but the regeneration gap between
the old and the new. To place the whole burden of psychic
and social salvation on the young, so that they must convert
their parents, their teachers, and their whole society is a
cruel hoax that this utopian humanism is playing on the
youth of America. Messianism is always a burden that breaks
the backs of those who bear it. The Messiah is born to die
the ignominious death on the cross. The cross is the acid
test of true Messiahship; it is cruel to nail the whole young
generation to the cross of our past history, to pierce their
hands and feet by our present dilemmas, and to ask *them* to
roll the stone away so that the future can be resurrected a
totally new reality. The whole story of Jesus Christ exists
in history to free us from becoming the saviors of the world
and to unburden us from the syndromes of self-salvation.
Humanism is antihuman because it taunts the crucified body
of mankind to come down from the cross; it calls upon the
sick to heal themselves; it trusts too much in the miracle
power of its own religiosity.


## Toward a Counter-Cultural Faith

In conclusion I will make two assertions which I expect a
Christian community might be willing to accept without
lengthy theological argument. The first is: it is a scandal that
the new religiosity thinks of itself in polar opposition to the
church. For if the new religiosity is a counterforce pitted
against the dehumanizing features of secular society, then
why does it regard the church among its enemies? The second is: not the young people as such, but the new people,
young and old, are the bearers of a message with hope for
the world. The two assertions bring out a glaring contrast.
The church is not seen as what it ought to be. It has become
a shadow of its own reality, perhaps a revolution against itself.

What is needed now is a counter-revolution, a revolution against the revolutionary denial of its true being in Christ as the great protagonist of the new future.

We as the church today must accept the messianic role (assigned by the Messiah, of course) that Charles Reich assigns to the new generation. We can take it because we don't have to prove our innocence. We exist in solidarity with all the sinful and godless people of the world. But we have heard the justifying word of our acceptance on account of the innocent suffering and death of Christ. That is the miracle of justification, the ground and source of our conversion to a new state of being. The most urgent need now is for the church to become a crucial experiment—an *experimentum crucis*. That is the process of the cross of Jesus Christ in history, crucifying the old to throw open a new dimension of time and to clear a new space for the arrival of resurrected reality in our midst. Then both secular Christianity and the new religiosity can unite in a new type of spirituality (cf. Chap. 6, below).

The eschatological forces released into history keep the revolution going for new things. The church is called to be in the midst of the struggle for the new. (1) For a new awareness, conversion to a new consciousness, *a new pietism,* if you please. (2) Also a new community, a new form of relation to others, interpersonal experience, overcoming the atomism of the nuclear family through a pluriformed communitarianism, of young and old and very old, children and grandparents, *a new monasticism* perhaps, incarnating the yearning for togetherness that is especially strong in a depersonalized society. (3) Also a new freedom, widening the range of free space in life, ridding ourselves of both the psychic and the social mechanisms of enslavement, domination and exploitation, a new world-liberation movement as the twentieth-century successor to the world missionary movement of the nineteenth century. The church is in dire need of *a new sense of mission.* It can be defined as liberation, lifting burdens, opening roads, expanding horizons, leading people out of slavery, out of exile, showing them the way home. (4) Also a new obedience, becoming a loving guardian of the earth as a potential new Garden of Eden—paradise restored—*a new eco-theology,* an earth mysticism, a new kind of asceticism in cherishing the beauty of the land. (5) *A new sense of transcendence,* of the presence of God as the unifying source and goal of the ecstasies of life we have been talking about, personal awareness, community with others, fighting for freedom and obedience to Mother Earth.

## NOTES

1. Harvey Cox, *The Feast of Fools* (Cambridge, Mass: Harvard University Press, 1969) .

2. Dietrich Bonhoeffer, *Letters and Papers from Prison,* trans. by Reginald Fuller (New York: Macmillan Company, 1953) , esp. the letters of April 30 and May 5, 1944.

3. Paul van Buren, *The Secular Meaning of the Gospel* (New York: Macmillan Company, 1963) , p. 2.

4. "The New Social Gospel Movement," *Dialog,* 5. (1966) , 135.

5. Ivan Illich, "The Church, Change and Development," *Dialog,* 9 (1970), 93.

6. *Chicago Tribune,* Sunday, September 14, 1969.

7. Theodore Roszak, *The Making of a Counter Culture* (Garden City: Doubleday & Company, 1969) , p. xiii.

8. *Ibid.,* pp. 43-44.

9. Charles Reich, *The Greening of America* (New York: Random House, 1970) , p. 4.

10. Theodore Roszak, *op. cit.,* p. 41.

# Part Two

# Counter-Cultural
# Concretions

# 6

# Spirituality

# of Hope

## THE QUEST FOR A NEW SPIRITUALITY

Shortly before his death Paul Tillich gave us his vision of a Religion of the Concrete Spirit.[1] He was not saying that Christianity was already such a religion. Instead, this projects a possible future for a Christianity that would fulfill the inner aim of the history of the religions of mankind, and achieve a synthesis of spiritual elements that St. Paul presented in his doctrine of the Spirit. The question of spirituality can be formulated this way: What does the Spirit do concretely? In personal life? In the Christian community? In secular society?

Today there are no clear answers to these questions. There is a widespread feeling that the traditional forms of Christian spirituality are not genuine. We hesitate to recommend a concrete form of spirituality to our children, and when we do, we hardly expect them to interiorize it. The spirituality on which our generation was nourished is perhaps enough to see us through. It will probably last our lifetime and then run out. But what will take the place of the traditional forms that are breaking down? I spoke to a Jesuit seminarian on his way to ordination. Jesuits have the obligation to do thirty days of the "Spiritual Exercises" of St. Ignatius, once before ordination and once after. He said, "Boy, I'm not looking forward to that again." Closer to home, we can look in on the worship life of a typical Protestant seminary. No matter how it is jazzed up, how new and experimental, how classical and beautiful, students stay away in droves. Even the professors would sooner take a shortcut to the coffee shop and

rap with the students. They don't do that with a good conscience, for they feel obliged to participate in a concrete
form of spiritual life. But they lack both the heart and the
discipline to put themselves into it. So the places that are
training men to be spiritual leaders tomorrow are astonish-
ingly void of spiritual life.

The word "spiritual" is itself treated like something from
a foreign language. We do not know what it means. It is not
uncommon to hear a person say, "Since I've had no spiritual
experience, I don't know what you're talking about." So it is
with great relief that students welcome the "secular theology." There they read that the lack of spiritual experience
is a healthy sign of their Christian maturity. All that pietism
is a hangover from the medieval past, with its belief in ghosts
and devils, and its preoccupation with questions of the soul
and getting to heaven. But presumably modern man has been
liberated. Harvey Cox's *The Secular City,* together with a
few of Dietrich Bonhoeffer's writings from prison, and we
could add Paul van Buren's *The Secular Meaning of the
Gospel,* heralded the rise of a new kind of Christian who is
radically a secular man, a man in tune with this age of science
and technology in an urban-industrial setting. The choking-
off of spiritual concerns can have the beneficial results of
redirecting human energies to building a better "city of
man." So seminarians feel, "Why waste your time in chapel,
singing hymns, smelling incense, and doing knee-bends, when
you can be out salvaging people from the gutters and the
ghettos?"

Traditional forms of spirituality are not being smoothly
transmitted to the next generations. This constitutes a challenge to us to interpret the cultural complex whose forces
make out of our lives a spiritual wasteland. Our interpretation does not arise from the perspective of a secularizing
theology, which says, "Gesundheit" every time our secular
society sneezes. Instead, it comes from an eschatological perspective whose key concepts are the prophetic power of
*negation* and the creative presence of *transcendence.* In old-

fashioned Lutheran language, that is "law" and "gospel," words that have lost some of their magic even in Lutheran circles.

The spiritual void in our churches reflects the consciousness of the times. In *The Greening of America,* Charles Reich postulates the existence of something called "the corporate state." In the structure of his thinking, this corporate state takes over all the functions of the devil in classical mythology. It is the one thing that is guilty of all the kinds of evil we experience today. Once we get rid of that, suddenly we'll break through to a beautifully green America, the symbol of youth, innocence, and fresh promise. That is all very appealing, but I'm afraid his demonology is a bit superficial. As Immanuel Kant said, "Evil is radical." It goes down to the deepest roots of our being. Before we dare talk so glibly about a new consciousness arising in America or anywhere else, among the youth or any other group, we had better take the full measure of the evils and the source of evil with which we have to contend. I am sure Charles Reich is right; the corporate state does exist. Once created to solve our problems, it has become our enemy. But an eschatological perspective will spare us the disillusionment that inevitably arises when, in winning the one victory we seek, we discover that evil continues unabated. Bishop Berggrav of Norway is reputed to have said about baptism: "In baptism we take the old man and put him under. But the old man can sure swim." Diabolism and eschatology are correlative. This means that superficial analysis will always lead to easy solutions.

We are in a bigger mess than Charles Reich imagines. Therefore we need a more radical analysis and a profounder spirituality than the new consciousness that he finds emerging in youth culture. It would be misleading for me to sound purely negative on his book, because, on most things, I am in his corner. However, its superficiality is appalling in light of an apocalyptic eschatology that reveals that our human struggle is not merely "against flesh and blood, but against principalities, against powers, against the rulers of the darkness of this world, against spiritual wickedness in high places" (Eph. 6:12) . After this verse, St. Paul goes on, "Wherefore take unto you the whole armour of God, that ye may be able to withstand in the evil day" (vs. 13) . Spirituality is a kind of warfare caught in the squeeze of forces between the eschatologically new and the diabolically old. It is this sense of what the fight is all about that in my mind accounts for the loss of spiritual power in the Christian churches today. I want to give an account of this loss.

*A*. There is no felt need for a concrete spirituality, and there can be none, when the power of negativation has been broken by the spirit of positivism. By the spirit of positivism I mean the objectifying consciousness which thinks there is only the world; it is just a neutral thing that we can handle like modeling clay, to make of what we wish through our science and technology. Man is just a part of the world; we can turn him into a lab experiment too, and make of him what the technocratic futurists schedule him to become. This power of negativation has always been a driving element in a dynamic spirituality. It functions psychologically as a contrast device, pointing out a glaring difference between the whole existing order and another one that has a higher right to be. Things are not just neutral; they do not just exist, to become objects at our disposal. Instead, they are seen as negative, as evil, as demonic, as destructive, etc. So spirituality is a way of negating the negative, of saying "no," of standing before oneself, and the powers that run the world, and saying something like, "Hell no, we won't go; we won't go for that." The point to be made is that spirituality is not all sweetness and softness and Pollyannish. To be something really positive, it has to be really negative—a fantastic paradox.

This is the way to evaluate the rise of monasticism in early Christianity. The ideals of the desert were, first of all, a sheer protest against corruption in the world and the secularization of the churches in the city. For that reason, the desert ideals have often been viewed as escapist spirituality. But there is another way to look at the matter. These Eastern monks went into the desert to do battle full-time against the forces of sin and Satan. St. Athanasius' *Life of St. Anthony* makes it clear enough that, at least in Anthony's mind, he was not running away from the battlefield. In that age it was thought that the devils had their headquarters in the desert, so he wanted to go where the action was. He and the other monks entered a life of renunciation, to thwart the devil's tactics. For the devil preys upon our desires and appetites, and has us at his mercy when he implicates us in so many activities that we become too busy and overwhelmed to put up any resistance to what is going on in the world. It is a sobering thought of Martin Luther that he prayed the longest when he had the most to do. In any case, it is important to see in the monastic movement the negativing process, the vital voice of protest against a church that was too easily accommodating itself to the economy of the world and the politics of the day.

It is this power of negativation that has become demolished in the totalitarian systems of life, dominating everyone in it through the mass media, mass education, advertising, making plastic minds in a plastic culture that leaves less and less room for those who really say "no." There are no outsiders; there is an unwritten law that everyone has to be an insider, all of us in the same bag. The melting-pot idea of America will bring a deadly sameness to us all. Our society is afraid of aliens, hostile to outsiders, and intolerant of any serious negations that reveal the demonries that control our lives and subvert our values.

Things are not significantly different in the American church. It is a part of mass culture, an organized system that enshrines the civil religion that Robert Bellah finds so useful in our society. True spirituality is lacking when there is no voice in the wilderness crying the forgotten truth of the absolute worth of one individual soul against the growing collectivism of the church as well as of our society. The monk was such a voice. The lure of solitude was a way of becoming free of the babble of voices of the world in the church and of the church in the world, each telling the other what they like to hear. No negativity! Instead, a complete reversal. Now the established order is okay; it is supposed to receive the positive accent. Those who are enough outside, looking back in through eyes of alienation, are made to bear the full brunt of the negative accent. So there is a lack of spirituality potent enough to say "no" in an organized system of alienating structures and functions and values. There are no monks in the church today to keep the negativing process alive.

*B.* But the negativing process cannot live out of its own negativity. A sheer "no" is impotent without an underlying "yes" to truth from which it gets the clarity of its vision. A lie is always living off the truth—like a parasite. Only an honest man can tell a successful lie. The credibility gap grows when liars get power and try to fake their lies as the truth. This means the power of negativation must be allied with the sense of transcendence. In the logic of Christian spirituality, the negative is most directly visible and audible, but the sense of transcendence is prior. I don't believe that a person can say "no" unless he has captured an alternative with his imagination. The strength of the "no" feeds on the power of transcendence. The early Christians said "no" to the imperial gods because they had been grasped by a new God who was the true God. They could say "no" to the present age because they anticipated the new age that was coming. It was their "yes" to the oncoming future of God's rule that freed them to hang loose in the saddle of this present order. Eschatology was the source of the life-style of refusal that characterized the early Christians—refusal to go along, refusal to get wholly plugged into the power systems of their world.

When Christians lose their eschatological hope, they fall into the grip of the here-and-now. It is the eschatological hope that keeps a Christian enough ahead of his time, always dancing slightly out of step with the tune of the times. The loss of eschatology in the structure of Christian spirituality meant that Christians found it more reasonable to enter the world of power-politics, to play by the rules of the game, and to enjoin the virtues of realism. The controlling ideology in both the world and the church is that what we need is more realists. We need specialists, men with efficiency and expertise—social planners, management directors, general staffs, and architects of the future. That is a lot of bunk. Poets and prophets, dreamers and holy men are totally irrelevant—except maybe for entertainment. Realism and pragmatism and empiricism in our culture have killed the speculative and poetic sensibilities that fantasize about the other world, the new world that is coming. Instead, our society operates on the one-dimensional premise that there is only this one world, this here-and-now world that is evolving, advancing, progressing ever forward until it develops into a bigger and better version of itself. There is no two-dimensional thing about it. From the beginning we teach our kids a problem-solving philosopy: think and do. We teach them to go "slow but sure"; we move along on a trial-and-error basis, so when the kids get big they will build SSTs or ICBMs and ABMs and build airports in the lake, and send ships into outer space, no matter if a slight leap of a free imagination tells us about the folly of such a future for our civilization. When the eschatological future loses its own dimension, but is squeezed into the mold of the present and the day-to-day movement of big business and big government and big everything else, then, as Polak says, "we have lost the ability to see farther than to the end of our collective nose."[2]

The rebirth of a Christian spirituality in an age that is bowing down to the god of this existing order, what St. Paul called "the god of this world" (II Cor. 4:4), will coincide with a full recovery of the eschatological dimension of the New Testament gospel. I say "recover" because the history of Christianity is also the history of its own secularization, that is, of a progressive self-de-Christianization. Christianity became more and more a religious adjustment to the status quo, a religious, institutional, sacramental dimension of the

present order, and lost its expectation of a future that could
bring a radical reversal of the existing situation. The kingdom that was expected as the oncoming power of judgment
and grace, of prophetic negation and transcendent hope,
became more and more postponed to a far-off thing at the
end of the whole show, and since history would go on for
a long time yet, eschatology had less and less to do with the
salvation question and with the spirituality that the church
fostered in its members. The church came to be seen, by both
insiders and outsiders, as a cozy corner inside the establishment. The early eschatological fever, expressed by the evan-
gelical "soon"—the day of the Lord is soon, Christ is coming
soon, etc.—is postponed to "some day," far away, off in the
remote future. In this way eschatology is not taken into spirituality. Spirituality is shaped and moved by other concerns.
At last eschatology in the West became replaced by anti-
eschatology and a capitulation to the present. Thus Ernst
Troeltsch could make the statement: "The eschatological
bureau is closed these days."[3]

It is a well-known fact of modern theology that a new
chapter was begun with the rediscovery of eschatology in the
work of Albert Schweitzer. Every new theological school has
felt obliged to give at least lip-service to this discovery, even
while destroying its meaning from within. Theology is still
hung-up on the eschatological question, standing at the door
of that bureau trying to find a key to get inside. The theology
of hope, the theology of the future, is another attempt to
unlock that door, to develop a genuine eschatology equal to
the challenge of our historical origins and the challenge of
the new horizon of man's experience in the world today. It
begins with a conviction that we have been confronted with
an array of pseudo-eschatologies. We find eschatology-sans-
eschaton, eschatology turned inside out, the realm of the
future minus the future, a messianic kingdom without a
messiah, a kingdom of God without God, etc., etc. The end-
result of this de-eschatologizing process is the secular theology,
the God-is-dead theology, and the like, which has eaten away

the innermost core of apocalyptic faith. This has left a spirituality with nothing to nourish it except the spirit of the times or the shallow life-styles of the secular world. It clings to the Christian faith minus the stumbling-blocks, without any form and content to the hope that lives from the presence of the ultra-human future that has arrived in the Man of Nazareth. If we remove the future as the source of our hope, we lose the resource of a spirituality that can sustain itself dialectically in the present—to live in the world but not of the world, because the source of life is the Spirit that transcends the world, as the absolute future transcends the order of this present age.

*C.* We are charting the cultural course leading to the spiritual vacuum in our churches. There is still another aspect to the destruction of negation and the absence of transcendence. It is the attack on myth, symbol, and ritual, expressed so famously in Rudolf Bultmann's project of demythologization. I do not believe that Bultmann *caused* the decline of myth in the church; instead, he was voicing what every preacher had already experienced. The myth has been broken and the symbols no longer flow spontaneously from our minds. We catch ourselves, hesitate, and then make an end-run around the symbol muttering some abstract utterance. The iconoclasm in the realm of the images by which we negate the present and celebrate the advent of the future of the Lord in Word and Sacrament proceeds first by making caricatures of our images. That is the process of fundamentalistic literalization. It happened when the spontaneity of symbolic language gave way to strained argumentation in defense of our symbols, as things literally true. The next step was to reject the literalized symbols as so much fabulous nonsense—unacceptable to the scientific mind of modern man. This cleared the field of the symbols of the Christian future, creating a vacuum. But human nature, like nature itself, abhors a vacuum. So it happens that Western spirituality gets rid of one demon, but seven more rush in to fill it up, and the last state is worse than the first. Now the future is turned against itself, not a beautiful future, but an ugly, chaotic, nihilistic, absurd, and revolting future. Such a future can only provoke anxiety, despair, Sartrean nausea, and horror of Huxley's "brave new world." Here the power of negativity is turned against the future, generating fear, hopelessness, and meaninglessness. So here and there we find an inverted spirituality: acquiescence in the present and renunciation of the future; indulgence in the moment, because—what the hell!—there ain't no future anyway, and even if there is, it's all about nothing. Here again, because the future has no dimension of its own, resourced by the death-transcending fountain of life itself, we are stuck in the world as it is. There is no exit. Spirituality that has to eat out of its own bowels must soon die of its own pollution. A spirituality of hope must be nourished by symbols of the future that participate in the power of life against death. We see that life breaking forth in Jesus' resurrection from the dead, and in that life we share in the immortal life of God. That is a main source of Christian spirituality for all seasons.

*D.* What we are really talking about is man. The loss of spirituality would not matter if it left man more sane and in better health. But when he loses spirit he loses himself, for spirit is the inner power of self-awareness and self-transcendence, infinite openness to all the newness and fullness and mystery of being itself—of God. So loss of spirituality is loss of self; it is the self getting lost in the world of objects and material entities which can be shoved around like boxes in a warehouse. We call that dehumanization, depersonalization. It is where the world is at today. Underlying it is a monistic world-view—a one-dimensionalism—in which the world is flattened out into facts without values, quantities without quality, broken up into bits and pieces without a whole, a body without a soul, mammon without mystery, a drama without a plot, a life without a future, sex without love, religion without faith, words without meaning. It is a deep prejudice of our culture, that nonmaterial things do not exist, that nonscientific statements cannot be true, that what is most visible, measurable, and controllable has the highest value. How is our society different then from an anthill, an insect society flying about with artificial wings called airplanes, a society highly mobile but going nowhere, just killing time, and being killed by speed. Days fly by, threaded together one after the other on the string of time, leading nowhere, because the chronological calendar has displaced the liturgical calendar in which time becomes sacred time, the passing of time a process of redemption, history the story of our salvation. Life that cannot be framed in terms of the historical myth of exodus, resurrection, and the kingdom of God is at a loss how to interpret itself other than as a chance collocation of atoms and the erratic explosion of energies.

Not knowing where we are at in time on this space-ship called earth leads to a deadly serious threat to human life. The spirit that opens to the future longs for a transvaluation of all values; the spirit that is confined to the flat world of facts and figures, to the language of mathematics, the logic of science, and the tools of technology simply cannot prevent the devaluation of all values. What American servicemen did to the poor villagers at My Lai, Vietnam, was not an isolated incident of a few specially barbaric individuals. It was the same "dirty hands" (Sartre) of the same filthy beast that operated the gas ovens cremating six million Jews, that now withhold food from the starving millions, that destroy the environment to enrich a few, that convert a free society into a police state, that jail the poets, electrocute the poor people, and poke fun at strangers in our midst. Our struggle is not against flesh and blood, but against demonic structures with power to destroy humanity. Our mindless technological machine is like a vampire that lives on the blood it sucks from children, or like a man-eating monster that needs a higher body count to satisfy the people and the politicians back home.

The problem of spirituality today is how to live a human life in the vacuum of a total structure that uses technology to promote mass-mindedness and materialistic patterns of

behavior. Our waking hours and our leisure time, our manual
activities and mental operations—all are invaded and dominated by hidden mechanisms of control, making people
want what they do not need, and leaving unsatisfied the basic
human needs. Jesus said, "Man was not made for the Sabbath, but the Sabbath for man." This saying must apply also
to the machine. The value of a human being has become
cheap. He is no match for the machine. He is of little self-
worth. *Homo faber*—man is a worker. But robots can do the
job more efficiently. With the loss of spirit, man can define
his meaning only in functional terms. But when the machine
usurps even those functions, there is no remaining source of
spiritual identity and meaning. So man, as a system of functions, with no overplus of meaning to himself and to others
and to God, a meaning that establishes an identity that
cannot be exhausted by his service to the organization, has
become replaceable. But a world in which persons can be
interchanged with things is a dangerous place for human
beings to live. Man is alienated from his world because the
technological world does not need him. He does not feel
unique and irreplaceable.[4] Like a thing, he is exchangeable.
The rat race in our society that causes human beings to
collapse of sheer exhaustion, or more literally of broken
hearts, is due to the drive to become the irreplaceable individual. There is an infinite longing in each individual to
have his meaning, his identity, his future secured on a lasting
foundation—on a "rock of ages." But here his world tells
him he is not needed. The most powerful man in the world
at the time—John F. Kennedy—was shot to death. There was
another, right behind, eager to take his place. Consider the
average man today. When he looks for work, there are hun-
dreds of others with the same credentials. The worker feels
he is becoming more like the things he makes; he beholds a
multitude of identical copies, all looking exactly alike. No
wonder he looks on himself as a replaceable part in a machine.

Man must respond to this fear of self-loss. As a human being
he needs to be assured of his uniqueness and infinite worth,

his irreplaceability. So he goes to work on his personality, to make himself unique, to cultivate his individuality. He takes on a certain "life-style" that gives him a peculiar appearance, a special badge of distinctiveness, a special combination of nonconforming manners and mannerisms. In a world that denies his uniqueness, the young man is bound to go searching for his lost identity as an infinitely beautiful, noninterchangeable, unique person. But this search for identity is a failure. It makes a wreck of people who try to retrieve their selfhood by pouring their souls into external and superficial marks of uniqueness. The irony is that these new badges of personal identification are equally part of the world of commercial planning, advertising, and exploitation. The "Who am I?" question cannot be answered out of this world that is itself so questionable. The answer can come only from the Spirit, a Spirit not of this world and not the spirit of the times.


THE SPIRIT AS ESCHATOLOGICAL EXPERIENCE

The progression of factors at work in the modern world—the denegativing process, the de-eschatologizing, the demythologizing, and the depersonalization—have devastated the traditional forms of spirituality. I do not think we can exaggerate the feeling of spiritual emptiness in the churches, the conquest of secularism. The institutions are a spiritless shell, a barren carcass. The bureaucracies that run them are like blind men leading the blind. The mountains of material cranked out by the office machines to stoke the ecclesiastical furnace may only be choking off the tiny tongues of spiritual fire coming up from below. On the other hand, as in the Acts of the Apostles, so now too, the Spirit has not left himself without witnesses (Acts 14:17). They are not always where we expect to find them. The Spirit blows *ubi et quando visum est Deo*—where and when it is pleasing to God.

A Christian doctrine of spiritual life must ask about Spirit. The Spirit blows into the present from the future of God, taking hold of life in the tension between diabolism and eschatology. We do not have the spiritual power within us here-and-now equal to the demonic forces at loose in the world. For our enemy is not the man in the White House, not the men in the Kremlin, not the Weathermen or the Minutemen, and not the class struggle or the Black-White thing. Spiritual insight does not underestimate the power of the enemy or commit the fallacy of misplaced identity. So we reach for a mythological symbol to match the reality of the enemy. "Be sober, be vigilant; because your enemy the devil, walks around like a roaring lion seeking someone to devour" (I Pet. 5:8).

The Spirit is eschatological experience. I do not wish to enter into subtle questions on the classical dogma of the Holy Spirit. Nevertheless, we cannot really make any headway on a Christian doctrine of spiritual presence without starting with a biblical-theological interpretation of the Spirit of God. God is not just ultimate reality—being itself. God is Spirit, and we experience God as Concrete Spirit, as Tillich says. We must succeed in drawing that into the horizon of our experience today as persons; otherwise it could be cast aside as an outdated concept. But before we touch down in our human experience today, to identify the operations of the Spirit within us, I want to make the point that for the New Testament the Spirit is eschatological presence. Only those born again of the Spirit enter into the kingdom of God. It is not enough to say, "Lord, Lord." A true confession of Jesus as Lord is only possible through the Spirit; it is a gift of spiritual insight. The earliest Christian community was filled with a Spirit-enthusiasm, linked to its conviction that the eschatological future that had broken through in the person of Jesus was now a spreading flame in history through men grasped by the Spirit. Ernst Käsemann has shown that this "enthusiasm and apocalyptic theology are hereby united in inner necessity."[5] The possession of the Spirit is the pledge, the down payment in the present situation, on the future of life that is promised to those who are in Christ Jesus.

A word of caution might be in order. Those of us who have learned our Christian grammar from Luther have become shy of "enthusiasm." Luther entered into conflict against the "enthusiasts" of his day, the spiritualists, the "Schwärmer." He ridiculed them as fanatical prattlers who "have swallowed the Holy Spirit, feathers and all." He was fighting on two fronts—against the objectivists on the Roman side, but also against the subjectivists on the Protestant side. The spiritualists had no use for the external means of grace: the letter of Scripture, the creeds of the tradition, the offices of the church, the physical elements of the sacraments. So he called them "the know-it-alls," for they claimed to have the Spirit immediately inside them, freeing them from all external instruments and sacraments. For these enthusiasts, history has come to an end in their own spirituality. That is exactly like the false enthusiasm in the church of Corinth, Paul's biggest headache. These Corinthian enthusiasts used the Spirit to put an end to history, and to glory in their superior spiritual state, as though, having the Spirit, they were no longer on the stage of trial and suffering. They are the spiritually snooty ones, who divide the body of Christ by their illusory perfectionism. They imagine themselves already across the goal line, throwing their hands in the air and dropping the ball, shouting hallelujah, while it turns out they are only on the twenty-yard line. In this way Christian spirituality becomes the spirituality of a mystery religion. In later history it crops up in gnosticism and in extreme forms of mysticism. Today it is sticking its nose into our culture through the influx of the spirit of Zen and the "mind-blowing" sacraments of psychedelia. The temptation is severe; it is spiritual backlash against the secularized church. Those who have been calling for a secular Christianity do not seem to realize that that is what they have already got. So the hunger for spiritual experience is driving people to seek it wherever it may be found. From a theological point of view, we have to say, "Déjà vu"; we've seen that before and we don't intend to follow these new spirits, to get our thrills from pills, or to become freed by speed.

The lesson we can learn from Luther is that there is authentic Christian spirituality, and then there is a pseudo-Christian spiritualism. The way to tell the difference is by the sign of the cross. Spiritualism is a flight from history, a premature exit into an esoteric realm of heavenly glory. Christian spirituality is faith on trial going the way of the cross in history. Spiritualism says the kingdom is all here; it is just a matter of being turned on, of turning inward, to see the face of the Lord shining in the realm of glory. That is a present eschatology, which says that the principalities and the powers have been dethroned, and we are already transported into another world of wonder and celestial light. St. Paul was of a different mind; as Käsemann says, he fought out his anti-enthusiastic battle in Corinth under the banner of apocalyptic, future eschatology. This means that the bloody body of mankind is still racked up on the cross of history, and we wait for the future to bring the final victory of the Lord and the redemption of our bodies. We are still very much in the thick of the fight; we are still sharing the pain of God in the world through the sufferings of Christ. We are still traveling as pilgrims of the cross bearing the pain of God on the way to the new creation, the new earth, and the new humanity, with a lasting future of a perfect freedom and a righteousness that makes all the broken bodies and shattered hearts into beautiful people through the resurrection they all inherit through Jesus our Lord and God's viceroy. It is indeed true that Christ now reigns; he is beyond the reach of death, but we are not. In his name and from his power we look forward in hope and longing anticipation for the end of death's lordship upon earth and the final defeat of the powers that still prey upon believers and unbelievers alike.

But ours is a spirituality of the concrete Spirit. This means that the Spirit makes really present the things that will be more fully realized in the future. While the men of the cross

look forward in hope for the final conquest of evil, and while
they now experience the pain of the world in solidarity with
all the suffering, their spirituality is also a reception of gifts
that bear the fruit of joy in the present. Spirituality is not
just a fuel to cook something up for the future; it is also a
table set with good things to eat in the present. Spirituality
is not only an anticipation of the future reign of Christ; it is
also a celebration of the present ecstasies of the Spirit, the
charismatic qualities of experience. Christians do not only
go forward in hope; they greet the advent and the presence
of the Spirit in their present. As long as this dialectic is maintained, between the finality of the future and its provisional
embodiment in the present, we will not succumb to the
spiritualistic delusion.

Then too, we will worship God with our bodies. We will
not try to struggle loose from our bodies by blowing our
minds. The Spirit as eschatological experience is experienced
in our bodies. We confess a body mysticism, a body spirituality. When you stop to think of it, where would you be
without your body? Paul says, "The body is for the Lord and
the Lord for the body." The body is beautiful; but when it is
a spiritual body, it is more beautiful still. A spiritual body
is this: a body in which the eschatological future of God is
already taking up residence. The body is the temple of the
Holy Spirit. There is no true spirituality that leaves the body
behind. The Spirit is bringing the power of Christ's resurrection into this dying world and into this concrete piece of
the world that is our body. The acid test of a Christian spirituality that takes the incarnation seriously is the body. The
body, not something else, is the battlefield of the two opposing power systems, each struggling to take hold of a person's
life by controlling the body.

The spiritual renewal that we hope for, the recovery of
spiritual vitalities in the churches, will not come from the
top. Nor will it come by making spirits soar into lofty regions
of abstract speculaton, by latching onto Zen and dabbling in
an eclecticism of the mystic, the occult, and the magical

phenomena that many in our culture are calling for in their quest for spiritual experience. Christian spirituality is not the ascent of the soul out of our bodies, but openness to the descent of the Spirit into our bodies. The spiritual hollowness and impotency in the churches can be reversed only by starting at the right place. If we want to get into the conflict between diabolism and eschatology, we have to get into it with our bodies. This is to reach back behind the monastic and ascetical models of spirituality that we see in the ancient church, as the monks fled to the desert. It is to reach back into the theology of the body, the somatic spirituality of the apostles, especially of St. Paul. This yields an ecstasy of the body, an ecstasy of the earth, in contrast to the body-denying discipline of the ancient monks, the classic example of whom was Simeon the Stylite. His disciple, Antonius, wrote, "When he walks vermin drop from his body."[6] He lived forty days in a cave with his leg bound to a stone by an iron chain, the point being to let his soul be free to fly by itself. He spent one summer not on the lake sailing a boat and sunning his body, but digging a hole in the dirt and burying himself up to his head each day. So he became famous as a saint. He was an extreme example, and yet he was the model of the life-style admired by all the others. St. Jerome writes with great admiration of a Christian who lived in an old cistern on only five figs a day. These monks were trying their best to be athletes of God. It is not enough to call it an exaggeration, and then quietly practice a milder version of the same thing.

A spirituality that takes the body as that concrete piece of the world in which the Spirit is establishing the rule of Christ and realizing the liberating power of his resurrection will be shaped by the body-theology of St. Paul. All the fullness of God inhabited a body, the body of Christ (Col. 2:9). God is Spirit, but always communicating his presence in the body. And we are members of that body. The bread we eat is the communion of the body of Christ. The salvation we are offered is the redemption of our bodies (Rom. 8:23); and the final hope for all men, now enemies of each other, is the unity, peace, and love in the body of the new humanity who is Jesus Christ our Lord. The renewal of spirituality will begin with the body as the concrete locus of the Spirit, whom we have defined as eschatological experience in the midst of the struggle against the powers of death and destruction. It will involve the material relation of the body to this earth as the ecological matrix in which the Spirit does his work.[7] He will work a new awareness, including sensory awareness; a new sense of freedom, expelling the *rigor mortis* in our bodies; a new sense of communion, of being together unafraid of each other's touch; and a new sense of transcendence, always open to the Spirit of God, who still has something new to say to the churches.

### NOTES

1. Paul Tillich, "The Significance of the History of Religions for Systematic Theology," in *The Future of Religions* (New York: Harper & Row, 1969), p. 87.

2. Fred Polak, *The Image of the Future,* Vol. II (Dobbs Ferry, N.Y.: Oceana Publications, 1961), p. 31.

3. Quoted by Fred Polak, *op. cit.,* Vol. II, p. 43.

4. An excellent study of this motif has been made by Dorothee Soelle, *Christ the Representative* (Philadelphia: Fortress Press, 1967), esp. Part One.

5. Ernst Käsemann, "The Beginnings of Christian Theology," *Journal for Theology and the Church,* ed. by Robert W. Funk (New York: Herder and Herder, 1969), p. 29.

6. Thomas Gannon and George Traub, *The Desert and the City, An Interpretation of the History of Christian Spirituality* (New York: Macmillan Company, 1969), p. 28.

7. See Chap. 8, below, for a discussion of eschatology and ecology.

# 7

# Apocalyptic
# Theology of
# Revolution

## The Etymological Chaos

More theology of revolution has been written in the last decade than in all the previous centuries of Christianity. In theology it is a neologism. In standard theological dictionaries the word "revolution" cannot be found. There is not one occurrence of it in biblical Hebrew or Greek. Could it be that as Christians we have no business trying to fit theology and revolution together? The common view among Christians is that the two should be kept separate; theology deals with the way of salvation; revolution with changing the world. The one is eternal, the other temporal; the one is spiritual, the other secular; the one is personal, the other political. These dichotomies have prevented theology from placing the revolutions of our world onto its agenda for serious reflection.

Another obstacle to a theology of revolution is the confounded word itself. What does it mean? Its modern connotation is directly opposed to its root meaning. Originally it meant "turning back to the beginning," like a revolving wheel. It was born in the matrix of ancient mythology, in which the whole planetary system returns periodically to its original position. So revolution was backward-looking, a return to the pristine beginnings. The modern view goes in the other direction. Its locus is not myth with its cyclical motion, but history with its forward movement; it is oriented to the future and looks for the new, the novel, and the never ever. So there has been a revolution in the word itself. The word has been converted. Now can it be baptized? It has been demythologized by being historicized. It is perhaps indirectly the impact of the Christian theology of history, with its high premium on a really new future, that has given the idea of revolution its changed profile in modern times. We have to consider this: if the modern revolutionary process is the prodigal son that has run away to a far country, can there be a homecoming? Can there be a reconciliation of Christianity and the revolutionary spirit in the modern world? Christianity has become a part of the establishment, whereas the revolution presses on to new and future dimensions of reality not yet manifest on the face of the earth.

A theology of revolution is in desperate need of a profound phenomenological analysis, taking into account the innumerable changes that have been called revolutionary. Even Plato would have difficulty in grasping the essence of all the phenomena that have been called revolutionary in our language. Just a spot check on everyday usage shows that our language is cluttered with a wide variety of meanings: the Copernican revolution; the French revolution; the American revolution; the Russian revolution; the industrial revolution; the technological revolution; the nuclear revolution; the triple revolution of cybernation, new weaponry, and universal human rights; the revolution of rising expectations; the youth revolution; the black revolution; the cultural revolution; the gay revolution; women's lib revolution—just where would the list end? Side by side there are peaceful revolutions and bloody ones, some more gradual, others very sudden. What, then, is the essence of revolution? I do not think it has essentially to do with bloody violence but, rather, with the objective changes that are subjectively felt in turning from an old order—the established way most people are used to—to a new order, which comes as a shock and with far-reaching consequences.

## THE ANTI-CHRISTIAN PASSION OF REVOLUTION

There is no end to the things that can be revolutionized—everything in religion, morality, and culture; anything from politics, to economics, to technology. A Christian theology of revolution is not limited to a single one of these. It is the nature of theology to think in total terms, to bring a perspective on the totality of things visible and invisible, of things present and things to come. It operates within a universal horizon of history; all things are viewed synoptically in light of their apocalyptic future. What we are really talking about is a biblical apocalyptic theology of revolution—a visionary preconstruction of all things in light of the eschatological future that irradiates from the Christ-event in history. If modern Christianity would have read the signs of the times in light of its own eschatological pointers, it would not have identified itself with the counter-revolutionary forces in the modern world. Modern revolutionary ideology has been decidedly anti-Christian and antichurch. The anti-Christian passion of revolution has been reinforced by Christians who crusade against the changes it calls for, and indeed accredit them to the Counter-Christ. Almost all American Christianity is united in an anticommunism, without seeing that the demons that rage in Russia and China are running loose in America with galloping ferocity. A cartoon captured it well, when the U.S. Army was caught spying on civilians. It pictured a Russian commissar showing the news clipping to his underling, and saying indignantly, "Copycats!" The polarization between Christianity and revolution has led to the dangerous illusion that the devils can be curtained off by iron or bamboo.

We can begin to break down this polarization by looking into the sources of modern revolutionary thinking. These sources lie in early-nineteenth-century philosophy of history, especially Hegel's. This philosophy of history became increasingly secularized as it broke away from its moorings in

Christian sources, especially of the apocalyptic kind. Hegel's philosophy translated the symbols of apocalypticism into concepts that show the dialectical movement of universal history. Inside its philosophical ovens there are live theological coals that keep them warm. On the two hundredth anniversary of Hegel's birth, celebrated in the Tübingen "Stift"— a house for Protestant students—of which Hegel was once a member, scholars debated the theme: What did Hegel do for theology? And what do theologians have now to do with Hegel? The address by Walter Schulz concluded: "Hegel cannot save theology, and theology cannot save Hegel." What the colloquium demonstrated, nevertheless, was that theology today dare not ignore Hegel, just as Hegel was more of a theologian than one usually discovers in the standard histories of philosophy.[1]

It is essential for Christian theology to recapitulate the nineteenth century. That is where we find the fork in the road. The established churches took the broad road leading to the defense of their own interests in the status quo; the revolutionary movement took the narrow road leading, as it hoped, to a brand-new world. The nineteenth-century German philosopher, Friedrich Schlegel, said that "the revolutionary desire to realize the Kingdom of God is the principle of modern history."[2] This becomes clear in Karl Marx. He believed that class struggles in history will lead to a world revolution, after which there will come a classless kingdom of perfect freedom for all. We have to insist upon a homecoming of all prodigal runaways in the modern world, otherwise Christianity is finished. So I speak about the need for recapitulation, to go over the ground again, to retrace our steps, to gather up all the insights and forces that became alienated from Christianity, to its own loss and diminishment. It is dangerous for Christianity to forget its own alienated offspring. Marxism is a child of biblical prophecy, no matter how estranged from its biblical origins it may have become. Christianity is a child of biblical apocalyptic, and it too has become profligate and disobedient.

The French say, "Il faut reculer pour mieux avancer"—
you have to go back before you can go forward. Recapitulation is necessary for both revolutionary thought and Christian theology, in order for both to construct a synthesis of a
higher order in the future. That would yield something like
what we are calling a biblical apocalyptic theology of revolution. The recapitulation process would mean that we have
another run over the ground of thinkers like Hegel, Marx,
Kierkegaard, and Nietzsche. If you consider the revolutionary
potency of the movements they inspired—communism, existentialism, and fascism—you have accounted for most of the
modern world. And in each case official Christianity has
found itself in full retreat, with much of its potential power
drained off by the other side.

Hegel brought to expression the idea that history is a
dialectical process leading to a total freedom. But freedom
presupposes the reality of reason. Hegel's slogan, the real is
the rational, is not a shallow rationalism but a vision of a state
of reality in which all possibilities have been fully realized.
In terms of scope and power it equals the apocalyptic vision
of eschatological redemption for the totality of reality. Somehow or other, official Christendom got itself ranged on the
other side of the issues of freedom and reason. It acquired
the image of being dogmatic, obscurantist, and antirational,
allied with forces that make for slavery and afraid of freedom.

Søren Kierkegaard tried to ring the bell to alarm Christianity into self-renewal. His outcry remains valid in behalf of the
solitary individual. Both Christendom and the grand revolutionary schemes have no real concern for individuals. Persons
are just cases that get lost amid the paper and pedantry.
Kierkegaard attacked Hegel because he saw Hegel as the
spokesman of middle-class Christianity, as though it were
the realization of the dream of freedom and reason.

Karl Marx took the opposite road coming out of Hegel.
Whereas Søren Kierkegaard called for radical personal faith
as the sphere in which the kingdom of the future—the eternal
—becomes realized, Karl Marx approved of Hegel's vision of

freedom and reason, but saw present history as moving toward catastrophe on account of its inner contradictions. Giving up the kingdom of God as the future of the world in motion, he proclaimed a utopia as the future of man without God. It is this atheism which has frightened Christians. Consequently they have failed to see that Marx's apotheosis of freedom in the future implies more theology than he cared to admit. To load the future with that much promise may be only a way of redivinizing a scheme of thought without acknowledging belief in God. Marx's idea that all history up to now is only prehistory is a familiar echo of the New Testament idea that what has happened thus far is a long way from the glory that is yet to be revealed (I Pet. 5:1). The center of gravity lies in the future for both Marxism and Christianity. Christianity expresses this investment of hope in the future in terms of the symbol of the second coming. As Christ was a new edition of Adam, so the coming Christ will bring a new edition of humanity more glorious than his first coming in the flesh—*kata sarka*. Where this symbol of the second coming of Christ is completely dead, Christianity has ceased to be the religion of the New Testament. To use Kierkegaard's language, it has become the antithesis of itself. It is then just another religion—*re-ligio*—tied to the past and dead to the future. Marxism has been a challenge for Christians to reconsider the priority of the future in their own interpretation of history and to stimulate impulses of hope that keep humanity looking for a redemption that is drawing near.

It was Friedrich Nietzsche who said that God has been entombed in the churches and Christianity has come to the end. This was longhand for saying that Christianity is dead. It has lost the future. The conclusion he drew is both interesting and consistent. If Christ is no longer the image of the future, then the future must fall into the hands of his counter-reality—the Counter-Christ. The coming of the Counter-Christ is the revolution to nothingness. There we have modernity creeping onto the precipice of nihilism. Nietzsche's message of anti-Christianity is an inverted sounding of the gospel. Who wins the future wins everything! If not Christ, then the Counter-Christ. Nietzsche's vigorous attack on Christianity is a way of screaming that the future cannot remain neutral, as it had come to be in Christendom.

## The Revolutionary Jesus

The recapitulation process can thus go back through the nineteenth century, gathering up insights from prophetic voices that opposed the Christianity of their day. But in the last analysis theology carries this process of recapitulation way back into the early church and its documentary sources concerning the historical Jesus. Was Jesus a revolutionary or not? However we may come out on our reappraisal of the revolutionary process in modern history, it will all be of no avail to theology if we cannot ground it in our knowledge of the historical Jesus. Friedrich Schleiermacher's criterion of what is essentially Christian remains valid today for every Christian theology: only that is essentially Christian that can be "related to the redemption accomplished by Jesus of Nazareth."[3] Was Jesus a revolutionary or not? As Oscar Cullmann has stated in his book *Jesus and the Revolutionaries,* the very last writing we have from his pen after the Paris revolution of students in 1968: "In all the current discussions regarding the relationship of Jesus of Nazareth to the phenomenon of revolution, the key factor is Jesus' attitude to the situation and movements of *his time.*"[4]

It is my conviction that Jesus was a revolutionary of a unique kind. In a revolutionary age a Christian will seek to embody the revolutionary life-style of Jesus of Nazareth. But what was that? Was Jesus a Zealot? The Zealots were the guerrilla fighters of Jesus' time. They were trying to bring in the kingdom of God by driving the Romans out. Religion and politics for them were all the same thing. Now there are those trying to promote a theology of revolution by linking Jesus to the Zealotist liberation movement.[5] So they lift up those clues in the Gospels which connect Jesus to the political agitations of his period. Hence, is it not the case that Jesus died the death of a political rebel? He died by crucifixion, the Roman method of execution. It was the Romans who put the inscription on his cross, *Jesus of Nazareth, King of the Jews.* If we follow up these clues, we will discover other evidences that Jesus was not so neutral in politics. He called Herod a "fox." He spoke about kings who oppress the people and yet want to be called their "benefactors" (Luke 22:25). He projected the kind of image that caused the crowd to want to make him king on the spot. Among his twelve disciples several were very probably Zealots. At least one of them was carrying a weapon when Jesus was arrested in Gethsemane. And the cleansing of the Temple was done with some force. Do all these clues lead to the conclusion that Jesus' revolution was of the Zealotist kind?

Oscar Cullmann says, "Not so fast!" There are many other clues that place Jesus against the political religion of the Zealots. He agreed with their hope for the kingdom of God, but it would not come in the style of the Zealots. Otherwise, why did he say not to resist evil and not to draw the sword, but instead to love one's enemies and to be peacemakers? Why did he accept tax collectors among his disciples and friends, inasmuch as they were doing business with the enemy? No Zealot would be doing that. So it seems that Jesus had a new style of revolution in mind. He did not come out endorsing the existing order, nor did he propose its violent overthrow. Jesus expected the kingdom of God to come and put an end to the present world order. Yet, he did not flee to the wilderness or attempt a premature flight from the world. Unlike the Essenes of whom we hear in the Gospels, and who may have been members of the wilderness community at Qumran which produced the famous Dead Sea Scrolls, Jesus took his revolution downtown into the midst of all the realities of the world. That is the meaning of the charge that Jesus was "a glutton and a drunkard, a friend of tax collectors and sinners" (Matt. 11:19). A picture of Jesus begins to emerge through contrast. He was not a member of the revo-

lutionary Weathermen or the Minutemen of his day, looking
for victory through violence; nor on the other side did his
relativizing of the world make him drop out, like the hippies,
running from the mainstream of life into pockets of isola-
tion. Looking toward a kingdom not of this world, he stayed
in its midst to keep it from closing in on itself, that is, of
absolutizing itself. His eschatology kept all things relative
and provisional.

Staying with the world on its way to the end he did not fail
to judge it in light of the kingdom of God. Consider injustice;
Jesus said, "Woe to you that are rich!" The differences
between the rich and the poor are completely unacceptable,
in full contradiction of the will of God. For this reason it is
practically impossible for rich people to inherit the kingdom.
One wealthy individual was told to sell everything and give to
the poor. This saying hit Francis of Assisi so hard that he took
it literally, setting an example that many have followed.
Others have said Jesus did not intend his statements to be
taken literally. They see him as an Abbie Hoffmann, using
extremist language for effect. But the first Christians did not
think so. They established a community in which the distinctions between rich and poor were demolished and the master-
slave relationship continued no more.

There is something very difficult to grasp about Jesus'
revolutionary style. The Marxist is quick to jump on it as
religious opium for the masses. The revolutionary groups of
today fault it for being nonpolitical and therefore soft and
irrelevant. They do have a point. For indeed Jesus did not
expect much in the way of institutional reform. He offered
no blueprint for a perfect society, come the revolution.
Instead, he turned to the individual and called meanwhile
for radical change. New possibilities would seem to arise
through a change of heart, the conversion of persons, rather
than through a new system of power structures. An exclusively personalistic interpretation of Jesus' approach is a
mistake, however. Christians have done their Lord no service
by making him a political eunuch for the kingdom's sake. It
is well known that Christians have tried to depoliticize the

role and message of Jesus in order to remove their own religion from the political spotlight. When the political authorities have suspected Christians of being subversives and enemies of the state, Christians have responded with the understandable but disastrous impulse of voiding Christianity of any political significance. Though it is true that Jesus was not a social reformer or political revolutionary, the message he preached drives a hard bargain in every sphere of life. The gospel is not politics, but there is a politics of the gospel.

In considering Jesus and politics, there is no forgetting the fact that his preaching and his action were not so safe and neutral that he could avoid running amuck the political authorities of the Roman Empire. The Berrigan brothers have been put in jail. Our jails are becoming filled with men who believe the gospel of Jesus Christ and act it out in the political sphere. They are tried in a court of justice, as Jesus was, and they are condemned as federal criminals, as Jesus was. We cannot forget that Jesus was no politician, but he died a political death for subverting and undermining the things that made Rome great. It is totally dishonest to state, as almost all the Lenten sermons in Christendom have stated, that Jesus was not guilty of the offenses with which he was charged. Of course he was guilty. He was a threat to the establishment. They had to get rid of him to serve their own interests. The courts were not corrupt; Roman justice was not inferior to American. "But they all condemned him as deserving death" (Mark 14:64). It was the death of a political criminal. It was this political event that the early Christians declared to be the salvation event par excellence. Indeed, Christianity is not political religion; but there is a politics linked to the eschatology that Jesus proclaimed and lived.

## APOCALYPTIC PERSPECTIVES

We have struggled to the conclusion that Jesus was a revolutionary of a unique kind. He was not a political revolutionary, but his revolution could not escape the web of political involvement. He had a chance to be a political revolutionary. That was his most severe temptation. The masses wanted to hail him a political Messiah. He did not accept the title because of its political image. The temptation stories picture Jesus in the grip of a political temptation. He could possess the kingdoms of this world, the devil said. But Jesus replied to him, "Get the hell out of here!" Jesus was fond of speaking like that. Once he said it to Peter in good Elizabethan English, "Get thee behind me, Satan" (Matt. 16:23). Peter had been harboring political dreams for his Master. As Cullmann says, "One is tempted by those things which are close to him."[6]

What is the matter with politics? Why did Jesus keep it at arm's length? Simply because it is too superficial. You have only to look at the politicians to become convinced of that. Political revolution is only surface revolution. It does not get down to the depths of human instincts and personal experience. Political revolutions kick out one gang of robbers and enthrone another seldom much better. Political revolutions lack the eschatological dimension.

It was Jesus' apocalyptic eschatology that equipped him to resist the political temptation as of the devil. There were those who wanted to make him king. But he answered, "My kingdom is not of this world" (John 18:36). He was bringing apocalyptic perspective into the political and revolutionary movements of his time.

Let us now look at some of the apocalyptic categories that made Jesus' revolution more than political. The first thing is the concept of the *totum*—total change. The new that is coming means a complete break with the present order. Politics presupposes too much continuity. Things are much more black and white in apocalyptic logic than in political science. In apocalyptic thought the great revolutionary reversal of cosmic proportions will be preluded by catastrophe, chaos, and calamity. This will also swallow up the revolutionary élite. None shall be spared.

The second is the concept of the *demonic*. There are powers and principalities of which political structures and programs are only representative. These demonic powers are like the "isms" that possess men's minds—like Nazism, communism, fascism, capitalism, racism, and the like. Apocalyptic eschatology operates with a sophisticated demonology, although many people write it off as a bit of outdated primitive mythology.

The third is that present realities are not all they seem, but are *signs of the times* pointing beyond themselves. Events have meanings, if only someone can read the signs of the times. This calls for interpretation of events in light of their future; that is prophecy. Those who are too close to the action usually know the least about what is going on. In the confrontation between Jesus and Pilate, who would have imagined that Pilate would owe his place in history to the man he condemned? Who would have guessed that time was being split between B.C. and A.D. before their eyes?

The fourth is that the coming kingdom is a pressingly urgent reality that calls for *radical conversion* in those who bear the message. You cannot wait to change until after the revolution. You must do it now."You must therefore be perfect, as your heavenly Father is perfect" (Matt. 5:48). One of the most hypocritical things about the revolution of American youth today is that they call for perfections in the system they refuse to realize in themselves, as though social change is more relevant than psychic conversion.

The fifth category is *unconditional surrender to absolute love*—love to God and to fellow men. This makes it impossible to love just those on the right side—or on the left side. You must not love the beautiful people and hate the pigs; you must not love the true patriots and hate the commies. Every man is a brother, even your enemy. The true revolutionary prays for the one who persecutes him. It is easy and natural to curse, hate, and kill. All of that requires no revolution at all but only to go with the adrenalin flow.

The sixth category is the *proletarian principle* of the gospel. This is the one that Karl Marx picked up. The gospel revolution penetrates a society and looks around for the poor. "Blessed are the poor"—not because it is enjoyable to be poor, but because there's good news for them. The kingdom comes when the blind can see, and the lame can walk, and the lepers are cleansed, and the deaf can hear, and the dead come alive, and the poor have good news preached to them. This prejudice for the poor does not divide humanity; it breaks down the division by raising up those at the bottom. The goal of this proletarian prejudice is the unity of mankind. All men are equal before God; now let them become so in fact. All are children of the heavenly Father; let them act like brothers. Here is the revolutionary power to abolish distinctions of color, class, and caste.

The seventh category is the *reversal of roles* that appears in apocalyptic imagery. There is irony, paradox, and esoteric logic in the kingdom of God. "The last shall be the first, and the first shall be last" (Mark 10:30). That is a great reversal. "Those who are exalted among men are an abomination in the sight of God" (Luke 16:16). Let the one who would be your leader become your servant. What is this but a new insight into the ordering of human relations? The back of the hierarchical model is broken with this reversal of roles. The entire meaning of being "number one" is altered. The aim of life is to excel in service of love to one's fellow men, not to make room for oneself at the top.

The eighth perspective is that when things seem most hopeless, they may be *birth pangs* of the future. The darkest hour can give way to glimmerings of new light. The deepest travail may be the pangs of newness. Salvation may come through suffering; pain and tribulation, anguish and misery, are not the last word. The eschaton is not death, though the earth became very dark on Black Friday. The eschaton is life, resurrection, the new being that rose into the light of Easter Sunday. So in spite of all, this is a time of hope.

THE COMING REVOLUTION

We could go on endlessly. Only a part of the apocalyptic conceptual system that Jesus used to define his revolution has been given here. But enough has been said so that we might make some critical applications to the present situation. Where might a person stand, what vision might a person hold, if he thinks and lives his way into the heart of the revolution that Jesus inaugurated?

The Christian is not committed to the system as it is. He is no defender of the status quo. He knows it will not last. So the meaning of time is its "meanwhile" character. What shall a Christian do meanwhile? First of all, he is to become aware of where he's at. That is faith—the revolution of the mind, getting rid of the false consciousness of mass-mindedness and putting on the new consciousness of a free man. St. Paul said, "Have this mind in you which you have in Christ Jesus" (Phil. 2:5). Find out where your head is at and get smart. Minds do not become liberated *en masse,* but one by one. Seize yourself; get hold of your instincts, feelings, and imagination, or you are doomed to be just a quantum in a mass technological society. Find out who you are, or you will become a stranger to yourself. For some time now we have been moving toward a mindless juggernaut in which "soul" values are ruthlessly sacrificed. Bring the revolution home to yourself; get your head changed. "Do not be conformed to this world but be transformed by the renewal of your mind" (Rom. 12:2). Before you can spread the seeds of life in others, they must begin to take root in the soil of your own personal life.

In the present situation the revolution will have to become more religious than political. Politics is helpless in face of the mass techno-society. Revolutionary changes in political structures do not reach down to the infra-structures of personal reality. In a perfect society of material satiety, what is there for the individual whose alienation is at bottom a sickness of the soul—sin, cynicism, and despair? In our society it is the children of the affluent, who have not personally suffered the miseries of poverty, legal injustice, and cultural deprivation, who are searching for a therapy of soul that political revolution cannot provide. Therefore, they are taking in ecstatic religion, to explore new openings of the mind. There is a new fascination for odd rituals, astrological lore, and mystical trips through psychic introspection and psychedelic experience. I see all that as the revolution in quest of religious depth.

The final question is: What life-style is most appropriate in a society controlled by the idolatries of military power, national pride, and material progress? What is needed is a survival strategy. An individual cannot do it by himself. Some are trying it. Like a Bronson, they head for the open road and keep going. That is lacking the communal dimension. It does not offer a real alternative that takes responsibility for the surrounding world. What is at stake is the future, not just of the restless youth, not just of the underprivileged minorities, but of the silent majority and the super-rich as well—the future humanity of all men. The most effective response to the American machine that has gone out of control is to create new communities of people who live out of a transcendently new human awareness. It is the same survival strategy that the earliest Christians tried—being in the world but not of the world, having one's being, but not being one's having. We need to blow holes in the system by finding ways to live as free men. This freedom means to live in accordance with our basic needs and to bring our demands into line with the interest of the world's peoples. Instead, the system neglects our needs, but creates artificial wants and demands. We have adopted a saying in our house that if it is on TV you cannot buy it. Big business controls TV, and TV controls people. It has been years since TV has advertised a single thing a person needs; indeed, he is usually better off without what is advertised. If that sounds extreme, it only shows how estranged we have become from our own humanity. There has never existed a society that has created such complicated superstructures on the basis of false consciousness. The greatest need is for people to free themselves from the illusion that they need what these structures provide.

Churches are not yet what they are supposed to be. If they are to keep the revolution of Jesus going in the world, they must project the future of the kingdom of God into the lives and communities of men in this world. Churches will become free territories; they must become spiritual sanctuaries where they help to heal the minds of men in an insane world. They must revolutionize the definition of what is sane and normal. The psychiatrist R. D. Laing has observed that "normal men have killed perhaps 100,000,000 of their fellow men in the last fifty years."[7] He says, "The condition of alienation, of being asleep, of being unconscious, of being out of one's mind, is the condition of the normal man."[8]

The churches should become communities of free men in the center of things. One sees very little of that happening. But as the system grows more fierce and diabolical, the need for freedom zones will become more urgent. I have a vision of a church bing renewed from its revolutionary source in the freedom of God in the person of Jesus. First, the church will become known as a place where the imagination is becoming de-alienated. It becomes free to serve the whole self rather than the system. The French radicals created the slogan, "All Power to the Imagination." Imagination is the power of divination—the mind in ecstasy beyond its ordinary everyday perception of things. Second, the church will become a friendship house for all people, especially for the aliens in the world. It will absolutely refuse to carry on patriotic propaganda for its own nation. Therefore it will appear subversive because of its transnational flavor. As a Christian community it will adopt the principle never to believe what the White House and the State Department say unless there are informed fellow Christians in other lands to verify the truth of it. We have no reason to believe that our leaders necessarily tell the truth. Christianity is an international movement. It is ecumenical or it is not Christian. National boundaries do not exist except as barriers to be transcended by free people. Third, the church will be constantly moving to bring liberation to others. It must believe that nothing is so contagious as freedom itself. Power-politics and street-fighting are neither Christian nor effective. Our society is on the brink of becoming a police state. There are secret files on people who sing freedom songs and carry peace signs. But Christianity is a conspiracy for freedom; its missionaries must cross state lines to spread the gospel of being free. Fourth, the churches will be demonstration centers for a freer life-style. They will be therapeutic communities, exploring all the ways to bring about an enlarged humanity. Here people will help each other to break down enslaving illusions, to find the symbols that can match the realities, to study the truth that makes men free. Fifth, when nothing else works, the celebration of life will go on nevertheless in the churches. There are times when you have done all you can. You are politically pooped out; your program fails; your dreams are smashed; you are in full retreat. So the strategy is to celebrate, to rejoice, to sing, to dance, to eat, to drink. St. Paul was sitting in jail. His revolution was now at the end. And he said, "Rejoice in the Lord always; again I will say, rejoice" (Phil. 4:4). That is the most revolutionary word of all, pouring joy out of a consciousness inspired by the absolute freedom of God.

We may wake up one day and find that the future is already here. There is eloquence in political cartoons, like the one showing a picture of George Orwell's book *1984*. The year 1984 is crossed out, and above it is written 1970. So also it may mean that the church of the future is already here, to cope with the growing repression in America. The church may be rising again in the sanctuary movement that runs from Boston to San Francisco. Some churches are declaring themselves sanctuaries for fugitives from political repression and the war. The sanctuary movement is not new. America itself was once a sanctuary for those who fled from the European wars. The North was once a sanctuary for runaway slaves.

Churches became places of refuge for the antislavery under-
ground. During World War II many Jews were hid away in
the convents of Europe. Today the concept of the church as
sanctuary takes on new relevancy.

The church as sanctuary is a counter-cultural possibility
in a time when the dominant culture becomes decadent,
demonic, and death-oriented. War, poverty, crime, mindless
technology, and ecological disaster are the most visible signs
of the beast. As a sanctuary the church will be an educational
center liberating minds, a cultural center forming new sensibilities, a liturgical center for outbursts of celebration, a
health center for the cure of spiritual disease, as well as a
refuge place for those who are running for life. The church
is called to be and to do these things—to have the perceptions
to cope with the perversities of our time.

## NOTES

1. *Evangelische Kommentare* (October, 1970) 3 Jahrgang, 10, pp. 599-
602.

2. Quoted in Arend T. Van Leuuwen, *Development Through Revolution* (New York: Charles Scribner's Sons, 1970), p. 261.

3. Friedrich Schleiermacher, *The Christian Faith,* ed. by H. R. Mackin-
tosh and J. S. Stewart (Edinburgh: T. & T. Clark, 1928), p. 52.

4. Oscar Cullmann, *Jesus and the Revolutionaries,* trans. by Gareth Put-
nam (New York: Harper & Row, 1970), p. vii.

5. Cf. S. G. F. Brandon, *Jesus and the Zealots* (New York: Charles
Scribner's Sons, 1967), who interprets Jesus' ministry entirely in connection with the Zealotist movement.

6. Oscar Cullmann, *op. cit.,* p. 39.

7. R. D. Laing, *The Politics of Experience* (New York: Ballantine
Books, 1967), p. 28.

8. *Ibid.*

# 8

# Toward an Ecological Theology

It has been said that the agenda of theology is set by the world. The truth of this statement is never more clear than when we consider the future of the material world from a theological perspective. Theology used to take the world for granted, as the scenic stage on which the precarious drama of human existence was being played out. Now the stage itself is being brought into question, and with it theology is being asked whether it has something to say.

Already we hear about something called eco-theology, a new term for a theology of nature that takes into account the present ecological crisis-consciousness. The average layman, like myself, on ecology hears a lot of apocalyptic talk about the death and destruction of nature. The end is imminent; the earth is being destroyed. Listen to the words of one writer: "The earth is in danger of destruction. Whether we lose our planetary home with a bang or a whimper, by the population explosion driving us to mad Malthusian adventures or by massive pollution slowly poisoning us all, is finally a matter of indifference. The very future of our world is now in doubt."[1] Is that to be chalked up to panic-mongering? Even before the ecologists told us about the impending doom of our natural environment, we heard from physicists that the whole material world is moving toward its death, the heat death that occurs through the increase of entropy according

119

to the second law of thermodynamics.[2] Such a prospect, however, referred to a future so far off that at most it signaled the ultimate meaninglessness of the material world. Both philosophy and theology responded to the prophecy of physics by relocating the question of meaning deep down inside the existential self and its relations to the world of other persons. Ecological prophecy, on the other hand, has moved the remote future of the material world much closer to the present moment, so that the anticipations of cosmic death become inescapably more existential. Thinking toward the future can no longer be existential in a way that leaves out of account the destiny of the nonhuman world. We are all in it together—all mankind together with all creatures and the whole creation. Theology brings a universal perspective on the living relations between man and the material world. In this chapter we will deal with some of the sources and symbols of this universal perspective, in order to lay foundations for a theology of nature and an ethic that rightly cares for the things of the world.

Theology today is on the move to recover a lost heritage. Since World War II it has made the transition from existential themes to political issues. Political theology, theology of revolution, theology of liberation for the Third World signal new directions that draw theology beyond the sphere of the purely private and deeply inward experiences of the individual. Theology is interpretation of the history of the world in light of its end. This represents a partial recovery of the universal scope of theology. Now theology must move on to an even fuller recovery by expanding its vision from the history of man to the history of nature. A whole century after Ludwig Feuerbach, theology still had done very little to turn back the scornful contempt that can be heard in these sneering words: "Nature, the world, has no value, no interest for Christians. The Christian thinks only of himself and the salvation of his soul."[3] Theology retreated from the outside world to the inside self and from the future destiny to the present moment, monotonously intoning the interior anguish of the moment-ridden self. This means that theology stood by warming its hands by the mystical fires that burn in the heart while the modern technological world was literally sending nature to the gas chambers.

There are those who lay a heavy blame on Christianity for our present ecological crisis. The famous essay by Lynn White, "The Historical Roots of Our Ecological Crisis," minces no words:

> Our science and technology have grown out of Christian attitudes toward man's relation to nature which are almost universally held not only by Christians and neo-Christians but also by those who fondly regard themselves as post-Christians. . . . We are superior to nature, contemptuous of it, willing to use it for our slightest whim. . . . Both our present science and our present technology are so tinctured with orthodox Christian arrogance toward nature that no solution for our ecologic crisis can be expected from them alone. Since the roots of our trouble are so largely religious, the remedy must also be essentially religious, whether we call it that or not.[4]

It is difficult to gainsay the Christian responsibility for the rape of nature. Where else does the idea come from that nature is there as so much dead matter to be made over to suit the nature of man, rather than to be dealt with according to its own nature? Where else does the idea come from that man is the sole measure of nature's utility, that it is so much raw material to be stuffed into the bottomless pit of the social stomach—a stomach that has had the bottom knocked out of it (Ivan Illich's simile)? Where else does the idea come from that the purpose of life is to work hard and produce much so that we can consume more and more and more—stashing away proofs of providence, divine blessings on those who increase and multiply? It is embarrassing even to mention these things, for it is doubtful that we shall soon, if ever, crawl out from behind the heap of destruction that a Christian-backed technological praxis has worked upon the face of the earth. Think of the megatons of explosives dropped by Amer-

ican planes on the soil of Indochina, bringing about a ruina-
tion of that land that an eternity of years will never heal! All
of this with hardly a whisper crossing the lips of the American
Christian establishment, its church presidents, episcopal
synods, official boards, and educational institutions.

A few outspoken ecologists have so little confidence in the
potential of Christianity to heal that they are looking else-
where for therapeutic measures. Some radicals from the
counter-culture are turning to Zen Buddhism, others in the
liberal tradition are returning to pantheism, which motivates
a reverence for the life of nature by divinizing all things.[5]
The reasoning is that if man and nature are like brother and
sister born from the same material womb, it may be possible
to see the living spirit of the universe permeating all things.
This could soften the attitude of man to nature. In saying
Nature with a capital "N" we are saying God. "Deus sive
natura," Spinoza said. Killing nature is suicide—and deicide.

It is not my intention to mount a polemic against other
more benign approaches to nature, whether they hail from
Eastern mysticism or Western pantheism. The friends of
nature need each other too much for that, because collectively
they are but a small voice crying in the wilderness of a scientific culture in which science plays the prostitute, kneeling
down to the highest bidder. offering her body of knowledge
to those who lust for power—government, industry, military,
labor, advertising, perhaps even the university and the
church. My modest intention is not to prove others wrong,
but only to rob the enemies of nature of weapons they think
they find in the sources of biblical Christianity.

## The Denaturing of the Future

The first step in gaining access to a holistic theology of
nature in the biblical sources is to break with the denaturation
of eschatology in modern Protestant theology. The denaturing
of the future comes to its zenith in the theological line from
Bultmann through Gogarten and Ebeling. I think it is a dead

end. Nature has no place in the eschatology of this theological school. The physical world has no eschaton in the demythologized language of hope. It is handed over to the analytic techniques of the natural sciences. Man and his material world do not have a common destiny. There is room for speaking of a history of God with man, after some manner of speaking, but not of a history of God with the material world. The eschatology of the Bible is the answer to the question: Where is the world going at last? What is the ultimate direction and goal of the world? The movement of the material world and the course of human history both advance toward a common point—indeed, the Omega-point—in the biblical picture of the eschatological future. But in the existentialist reduction of hope-language, man stands alone, like the fabulous cheese in the children's nursery rhyme. It is not the Bible, but first gnosticism, then in modern times Kantianism and existentialism,[6] that dissolve the covenant of God with nature and press Christian faith to exclude the material world from its hope for the future and from being an intrinsic relation to the eschatological Christ.

In Christian existentialism the eschatology of the Bible is thinned out to mean scarcely more than an existential stance of openness toward an ever-receding empty future. The symbols of the eschatological future are lavished on the solitary exister. The natural and material worldly contents of these symbols are looked upon as inauthentic utterances of faith. Friedrich Gogarten followed Bultmann in the denaturing of the future. Christian hope looks forward to the pure futurity of God.[7] This is a futurity that is absolutely other than the future of the world. The physical world of matter outside us may have a dark or a bright future of its own, whatever the scientists tell us, but this massive future has nothing whatsoever to do with the pure futurity of God. Here Gogarten is trying to make good the eschatology of the New Testament; instead he makes a fatal error. He sets the future of God and man against the future of the world. The core of eschatology is what fits into the faith of the individual. The images of hope in biblical eschatology that concern the future of the cosmos are flicked away as leftovers from late-Jewish apocalyptic eschatology. All that hope for a new world is left to perish with ancient mythology.

Gerhard Ebeling goes in the same direction. Indeed faith and the future belong together, but this future of faith is totally other than the future of the world. With respect to the future of the world we may make our conjectures and calculations, we may invest in insurance policies and horoscopic forecasts. But with that kind of future, the world's tomorrows and the days after tomorrow, faith has nothing to do. Faith instead is open to a future which in the end is nothing else than faith itself. So Ebeling says, "Faith does not 'have' a future, it is the future."[8] Again and again we are told that this futurity of faith does not comprehend a new condition of the world, a new set of facts, a new earth, and things like that. Faith should not be led astray by the "conglomeration of mythological views of the world" that we find in the Bible.[9]

The upshot of the theological trend we have been delineating—including Bultmann, Gogarten, and Ebeling—is that the gospel becomes good news to men but bad news for the world. Nature and man are not synergized by the unifying power of the gospel, but the split between the self and the world continues indefinitely in gnostic fashion. There is another track in modern theology, however, that veers away from the existentialist extraction of man from his material world. Man is in continuity with matter even while transcending it. Nature is not there only for man. Man is a very recent newcomer in the history of creation; he has no reason to believe it is all there for him. A new theology of nature—that is something else than natural theology—is now more possible with the renaissance of apocalyptic ideas in the Bible.[10] The rise and development of a false Christian attitude toward nature coincided with the dismissal of its own apocalyptic beginnings. Therefore we are at least in the right to ask whether the glory of nature in biblical apocalyptic may not shine some of its light into our darkened understandings.

## THE APOCALYPTIC VISION OF THE WORLD

All contemporary theologians who have developed the outlines of a theology of nature are in some way indebted to the cosmic eschatology of the Bible. Cosmic imagery in biblical eschatology arose most explicitly in the apocalyptic writings. This is the original source of the cosmic categories of thinkers like Teilhard de Chardin, Nicholas Berdyaev, Paul Tillich, and Ernst Bloch. The basic contribution of apocalyptic theology was to project one eschatological synopsis of the history of mankind and the movement of the material world. It is not customary to place Teilhard's thought against the backdrop of apocalyptic eschatology, because the main lines of his thought were evolutionary in a way never dreamed of by the biblical writers. Nevertheless, apart from the means the end is the same. Ultimately the forward movement of the material world and the history of personal and social life converge on the same ultimate goal. The breakthrough of all elements (the universal motif) of the world into an infinite fulfillment does not occur without pangs and agonies on the threshold of the parousia (the crisis motif), and so Georges Crespy rightly observes: "the eschatology of Teilhard is not without apocalypticism."[11]

This mention of Teilhard can encourage theology to attend to its own apocalyptic origins, to recover from there a cosmic vision that incorporates the future of man and the world within the horizon of their common destiny in the eternal plenitude of God. Ernst Bloch provides a similar challenge. Materialist though he be, he is not a mechanistic materialist of a vulgar sort. The world is matter becoming spirit through inner self-transcendency. So he says, "Nature like history becomes truly manifest within the horizon of the future."[12]

An all-too-common view of apocalyptic is that out of its pessimism it forfeits the whole world to utter annihilation, while the souls of the saints float off in another world beyond the clouds. No doubt the apocalyptists did oscillate between moods, sometimes exuding despair for a world wholly unfit for the future kingdom, yet often leaping beyond that despair to a hope that grasped the idea that the whole universe of reality—the entire span of human and cosmic history—is being drawn into the final unity of God. Not only individual men, not merely mankind as a whole, but the whole creation, including the stars and the planets, the winds and the waves, the rocks and the flowers, the animals and even our bodies, is headed toward a total salvation. H. Paul Santmire is right on the mark when he writes in *Brother Earth*:

> The biblical writers do not see nature slipping away into nothingness at the Final Day. Rather they affirm that it is to be renewed and transformed, as men will be renewed and transformed. God has a plan for nature as well as for man; he has a history with nature as well as with man. He creates it so that he might bring it to fulfillment, not only in order to provide the scenery for human history. Man and the whole of nature look forward to consummation in the Kingdom of God; both are established at the very beginning with reference to that Future.[13]

If man's attitude to nature is a religious problem and if the ecological crisis calls for a radical change of consciousness inspired by a total religious perspective, here in the cosmic eschatology of the biblical writers we can find symbols of renewal for the atrophied imagination. In a brief sketch we will enumerate some symbols and motifs that can serve as building materials for a new theology of nature.

First, nature has a glory and a beauty wonderful to behold. Nature speaks. "The heavens are telling the glory of God." Nature is not that Newtonian world enchained by a rigid system of laws that cannot be broken. So it is proper that the sheer wonder evoked by the miracle of nature be converted into pure worship of the God of nature, for "the firmament showeth the work of his hands." Sam Keen has written an *Apology for Wonder* grounded in this perception that a God who is not the Lord of nature will not last for long as the Lord of history either.[14] The prelude to the death of the God of history is the death of the God of nature. The implicate of

confessing the Lordship of One God is the universal extension of his meaning to the totality of all reality, visible and
invisible, past, present, and future.

Second, the glory of nature is often eclipsed by the tragedy
of nature. Nature is depicted as having fallen, now existing in
a state of bondage, moaning and groaning under a tyranny of
demonic powers that will not release it to its highest good.
That is why it is such a threatening environment for man,
why there is a continuing warfare between man and nature.
In the words of that favorite philosopher of the White House,
Eric Hoffer, "the context between man and nature has been
the central drama of the universe." Humanization has meant
liberation from nature, its "floods, fires, tornados, blizzards,
hurricanes, typhoons, hailstorms, sandstorms, earthquakes,
avalanches, eruptions, inundations, pests, plagues and fam-
ines."[15] The apocalyptists experienced these terrors of nature
with keen sensibility, and said the world has fallen. The fall
is not only an existential phenomenon, making man a stranger
to himself and an enemy of others. It is a cosmic event affect-
ing the whole structure of things in heaven and on earth. It
is the snake in the grass that first puts the evil thought into
the mind of a woman; it is the cursing of the ground that will
make man's life unmitigated toilsome drudgery and bloody
sweat. It is the promiscuous relations of the angels of heaven
with the daughters of men that beget a race of monsters
spreading evil in the world. We are not so far from this way
of thinking today, with the surprising resurgence of astrology.
I read an article the other day in a Philadelphia newspaper,
which said, "Watch out, the new thing in the 'seventies will
be witchcraft, and lots of it." Scientific thinking is really not
able to assuage the desire of the imagination for symbols of
mystery that point to the fateful powers that influence the
course of human events, and that ancient mythology pictured
as flying and hovering elusively in the air. Therefore, men in
the modern world who make the attempt to think in strictly
scientific terms finally have recourse to such mythical terms
as the "id," the "collective unconscious," the *élan vital*, and

the "Omega-point." These are transpersonal powers of being. The apocalyptists saw no way of grasping the dynamics of life and its forms of meaning except in terms of such symbols as "good and bad angels."

Third, as the glory of nature is linked to the beauty of God, and as the tragedy of nature is linked to the sin of man, so also the renewal of nature is linked to the dawning of the coming messianic era. The age of the Messiah means getting rid of the demons in the world. It is a time of peace in the animal kingdom: "The wolf will dwell with the lamb, and the leopard lie down with the kid" (Isa. 11:6–7). It is a time of harmony between men and animals, and we could add, a time for the greening of nature, for a carpet of the greenest grass to spread across the ruined landscape of our ugly cities, and to turn the garbage dumps into garden cities where men can live, happy, healthy, and at home with each other.

Fourth, the apocalyptic tradition of cosmic symbolism is extended into the New Testament, with special modifications in the medium of Christology. The Synoptic Gospels, once thought to present a simple picture of the historical Jesus, are as a matter of fact framed by the cosmic scope of christic meditation. The healings of this man are eschatological miracles in which the demons are put to flight; he wins a victory over Satan, and sends out signals that the new age is already breaking into nature and history. "Even the winds and the waves obey him," it is written (Matt. 8:27; Mark 4:41; Luke 8:25). The central activity of the Christ is breaking the power of the demons which keep the world enthralled.

A man's body is his bond with the natural world, so the power struggle is taking place in the body. There is no merely spiritual redemption. Spirit power is freeing up of bodies. Man does not only live in nature; nature lives in him, and the moment he is separated from the living body of nature, he is pronounced dead. The human body is the place where the struggle for a new view of nature will be won or lost. The recovery of the "whole man" theme will be the point of renewing the "whole earth" theme. Anthropology must be the key to ecology, because the body is of a piece with man's physical environment.

Fifth, there is no eschatology for man or matter without passing through the ordeal of judgment and death. There is no painless access to the kingdom of God; all things must go the way of the cross; all things must be incorporated into the death of the Christ before sharing his everlasting future. In this way the principle of death in the cosmos is broken. The philosophers of the Enlightenment had difficulty with the idea of the resurrection; they believed it contradicted the laws of nature. But the hope for a new creation is not a violation of the old, but a prayer for its completion and perfection. The Messiah did not come to destroy but to fulfill. In the words of Thomas Aquinas, "Gratia non tollit sed perfecit naturam." Richard R. Niebuhr writes, "The Resurrection of Christ does not violate nature, but only death."[16] And in his *Theology of the Resurrection,* Walter Künneth sums up his theology of nature this way: *natura spirat resurrectionem.*[17] The life-and-death process in nature is reversed into a death-and-life rhythm in the resurrection. The resurrection is not a symbol of what is going on in nature as much as nature creates symbolism for the truth of the resurrection that ultimately reality shall not end in the abyss of nothingness but in the fullness of life eternal. As Paul put it, "The last enemy to be destroyed is death" (I Cor. 15:26). A theology of nature that will not lead us back into despair must take its cue from the hope born of Easter. Nature has a double face. The face that turns to the morning of resurrection rather than the one that turns to the evening of death receives the shining light of God's countenance and the glorious benediction of his *doxa*. Not death but life is the eschaton of all things—for Christ's sake. That is the ultimate hope of the Christian apocalypse in the symbolism of the first Christian century.

Is such a hope too much for us today? Are we too realistic, pessimistic, or empiricistic to bless nature with a hope that

God will keep his covenant with nature? And if so, can there be any real hope for man if man has given up hope for nature? Oetinger the mystic said: "Corporeal being is the end of the ways of God." I would like to appropriate this concept for our purpose to mean that just as the body is the concrete expression of spirit, so ethics is the concrete expression of an eschatological vision that embraces hope for the future of the material creation.

## A NEW ETHIC FOR AN OLD WORLD

A contemporary biologist, Edmund W. Sinnott, tells us that the future of man and his world is made out of the stuff of his dreams. He writes that the "lesson to be learned from the biology of man's spirit is that what will decide his destiny are the goals of his desire. Hope for him depends on their being raised so high that he will lift himself upward in achieving them. He cannot be driven. He cannot be coerced. But he can be *led* by the drawing power of his desires."[18] Similarly C. F. von Weizsäcker, the German physicist, says that the future of man hinges on the question of power. "Power has to do with the future. External power holds future events in its hands. In this sense, too, the gods have been considered powerful."[19] According to the Bible that power is within man as the image of God in which he is created. What does this mean? "In non-mythical terms: the image in which God appears to man does not show what man is but what he might be."[20] In addition to the voice of the biologist and the physicist we can listen to a sociologist, Fred Polak: "That man exercises influence over his future through his image of the future is only half the truth. The other half is that the future itself in its turn exercises a special influence over man and his images of the future."[21] These and many other hints in our culture lead us to emphasize the futurist perspective of the Bible as the basis of a Christian ethic that comes to grips with the crises of our times.

Ethics is a matter of deciding and doing what is good and what is right in the world. What is good and right in the world is determined by what is the well-being of the world. The eschatological perspective advances the idea of the well-being of the world into the zone of the new being of the world. Man must act toward nature to bring out the promise of nature, in every way to approximate the vision of the renewal of nature in the kingdom of God. The vision of animals at peace in the kingdom means that man must practice that peace already in the animal kingdom. Laws against cruelty to animals are signs of a healthy attunement to the new being of nature. The ethical maxim is: So act as though the aim of your action coincided with the inner drive of every creature toward fulfillment in the kingdom of God. The contents of ethics are principles of action calculated to embody as concretely and approximately as possible the realities of the future kingdom in the provisional and transitory contexts of the present. This is situation-ethics under the impact of eschatological goals. In this view the ethical task is to let the eschatological promise reach as much fulfillment as possible under the existing conditions. Utopian trends in behalf of nature can be set in motion out of an eschatological future that promises to make the past live again and bring back to life the things that are dying. It happens that the utopia of today becomes the working model of tomorrow. Norman Thomas used to complain that even the Republicans now vote for the social policies he pioneered and for which he was written off as a fuzzy-headed idealist. Looking to the other side of the coin, we see the leading actors of today following the script of the dystopias of yesterday, Huxley's *Brave New World* and Orwell's *1984*. This shows that there is life-power and life-style emanating out of our desires and dreams of the future. Eschatology pays off in ethics; it is the ever-fertile source of hope for meaningful life and action in a dying world. The world does not carry the future within itself as an imperishable mode of being from the beginning. The death of nature and the suicide of mankind are real possibilities. The future of life is a gift that is given to the world on the other side of its dying.

What the world needs now are missionaries of the earth who themselves live out of the future of life, pouring themselves into this world as living sacrifices well-pleasing to God and his creation. What the world needs now are not more producers and consumers of earth's resources, but more lovers who will dress the garden and name the animals one by one, respecting nature's thorns and thistles, its teeth and nails, so it can defend itself. But men with weapons of science and technology have risen up like devils to rape and murder the body of our "sister nature."[22] Man has become the Antichrist of nature, wresting it from its Creator, taking it into captivity. Man has invented an ethic of the survival of the fittest, and has proceeded to condemn the weakest of beings to death. Man is the most savage of all the animals. The demons of nature are raging in his heart. His poison is deadly. He aims to kill. When the floods were coming and God said all would perish from the earth, Noah brought thousands of animals into the ark, but only seven people. That shows a delicate sense of ecological wisdom. But now man is polluting the earth with his population and driving swarms of living creatures out of existence—the birds that fly above the earth, the fish that swim in the lakes, the beasts that run in the forests. In recent centuries man has treated nature as his enemy and has attacked it like a beast of prey. But von Weizsäcker says, "Such an animal will go on spreading until its prey is eaten up, then it will starve to death. How can we prove that man is not like this animal."[23] The thought has come to some that man is obsolete—unless he repent of his ways.

I have this story from my friend Olav Hartman, the Swedish novelist, who got it from Romain Gary. It concerns captives in a Nazi concentration camp who had to carry sacks of cement from one place to another. One day one of the captives bent down to help a scarabaeid (a beetle) which had fallen on its back and couldn't move. Soon all the prisoners were bending over, taking part in "operation scarab." But the sergeant commanding the captives raged and tried to kill all the scarabaeids he could see. We are at that point in the history of man in nature. The time has come, Hartman says, for many "operations scarab." That is bringing the future of the world we hope for into the crisis of the world we care for. That is ethics in the process of realizing eschatology— acting now in the light of promise and future hope. Conversely, an eschatology that ultimately negates the future of the material world will retroactively generate an ethics of world-negation. A fatalism will reign; people will say, "Après nous le déluge!" Antifuturism will take its toll. People will work for the future only if they are lead to believe in it. An eschaton that brings only death and negation in the future will send its poison and pollution into our present. That is why I said, in agreement with White, that a culture's attitude to the world of nature is at bottom a religious problem. The present is the time in which a culture acts out its hopes. To have a different world we must dream a different dream. Christian eschatology is such a dream. What we are plagued with in our culture is a nightmare. Religion is the sphere in which the ultimate choice is made—a dream that matches the promised reality of God's word, or a nightmare that lengthens steadily into a future filled with the deliriums of our time.

## NOTES

1. H. Paul Santmire, *Brother Earth, Nature, God and Ecology in Time of Crisis* (New York: Thomas Nelson, 1970), p. 6.

2. C. F. von Weizsäcker, *The History of Nature* (Chicago: University of Chicago Press, 1949), pp. 50ff., 70ff.

3. Ludwig Feuerbach, *The Essence of Christianity*, trans. by George Eliot (New York: Harper & Row, 1957), p. 287.

4. Lynn White, "The Historical Roots of Our Ecologic Crisis," in the Appendix of Francis Schaeffer, *Pollution and the Death of Man* (Wheaton, Ill.: Tyndale House Publishers, 1970), pp. 111, 114.

5. Cf. Richard Means, "Why Worry About Nature?" in the Appendix of Schaeffer's book, *op. cit.*, pp. 117ff.

6. This point has been demonstrated with impressive detail by Allan Galloway's book, *The Cosmic Christ* (New York: Harper & Row, 1951). This book was ahead of its time; at least, it is time to give it a new reading. It was one of the few books giving apocalyptic thought a favorable interpretation in the 1950s, the heyday of neo-orthodoxy and existentialism.

7. Friedrich Gogarten, *Verhängnis und Hoffnung der Neuzeit* (Hamburg: Siebenstern Taschenbuch Verlag, 1966).

8. Gerhard Ebeling, *The Nature of Faith,* trans. by Ronald G. Smith (Fortress Press, 1961), p. 175.

9. *Ibid.*

10. A most promising beginning is sketched by Wolfhart Pannenberg, *Erwägungen zu einer Theologie der Natur,* co-authored with A. M. Klaus (Gütersloh: Gütersloher Verlagshaus Gerd Mohn, 1970).

11. Georges Crespy, *From Science to Theology, the Evolutionary Design of Teilhard de Chardin* (Nashville: Abingdon Press, 1968), p. 142.

12. Ernst Bloch, *Das Prinzip Hoffnung* (Frankfurt/Main: Suhrkamp Verlag, 1959), p. 807.

13. H. Paul Santmire, *op. cit.,* p. 92.

14. Sam Keen, *Apology for Wonder* (New York: Harper & Row, 1969), pp. 107-113.

15. Quoted by Sam Keen, *op. cit.,* pp. 133-134.

16. Richard R. Niebuhr, *Resurrection and Historical Reason* (New York: Charles Scribner's Sons, 1957), p. 77.

17. Walter Künneth, *The Theology of the Resurrection* (St. Louis, Mo.: Concordia Publishing House, 1965), p. 179.

18. Edmund Sinnott, *The Biology of the Spirit* (New York: Viking Press, 1955), p. 170.

19. C. F. von Weizsäcker, *op. cit.,* p. 181.

20. *Ibid.*

21. Fred Polak, *The Image of the Future* (Dobbs Ferry, N.Y.: Oceana Publications, 1961), Vol. I, p. 51.

22. A term used by Joseph Sittler in his famous New Delhi address entitled "Called to Unity," in 1961.

23. C. F. von Weizsäcker, *op. cit.* p. 170.

# 9

# Eschatology
# and the Future
# of Religions

At the end of his career Paul Tillich was beginning to sketch out the elements of a new theology of the history of religions. He did not get very far because he realized that "we need a longer, more intensive period of interpenetration of systematic theological study and religious historical studies."[1] But he added, "This is my hope for the future of theology."[2] Are there any signs that his hope is now being fulfilled? I think there are: first, the history and the phenomenology of religions are growing disciplines of scientific study, and second, systematic theology is recovering the theme of eschatology which originally pulled the Christian faith into a missionary encounter with the world religions.

There is no way to have a genuine eschatology without making it work within the history of religions. The weakening of eschatology will sooner or later betray itself as indifference to the non-Christian religions. This indifference can take either one of two forms: the non-Christian religions can be rejected as having nothing to contribute to revelation and salvation, or they can be accepted as equally valid and fulfilling in their own way as Christianity.

Christianity is an eschatological religion that must make good its claim to universal validity within the stream of history, including the history of religions. That is the foundation of the Christian mission. If Christianity were not an eschatological faith it would have no need to bear the cross of humiliation for the failure of its mission to the nations.

Karl Rahner rightly states: "The fact of the pluralism of religions, which endure and still from time to time become virulent anew even after a history of two thousand years, must therefore be the greatest scandal and the greatest vexation for Christianity."[3] The Christian mission is the means by which an eschatological faith projects its own future into world history as the ultimate unifying future of the plurality of religions. The mission is the laboratory in which the presence of the eschaton in Jesus and in the apostolic kerygma is combined with the religious hopes and symbols of mankind, thus producing the history of Christianity as a dialectical synthesizing process on the way to the absolute future of the kingdom of God.

Tillich was fond of quoting a famous saying by Adolf von Harnack, the greatest Protestant historian who ever lived: "Christianity in itself is a compendium of the history of religion."[4] Christianity is more of a syncretism than its orthodox dogmaticians have been willing to acknowledge. The chief dogmas of orthodoxy, namely, Trinity and Christology, are themselves a result of a far-reaching Hellenization of Christianity, and can be interpreted adequately only within a postbiblical horizon of religious experience and philosophical understanding. In its classical period Christianity moved openly and creatively within the wider horizon of the total religious situation, knitting into its own fabric colorful threads of feeling and thinking spun out of the pagan religious environment. The naturalness with which it went about doing this arose out of confidence that its message carried the hope for a fulfilling future of all the religions of mankind. There is a common fear that the absolute claim of Christianity will make it rigid and narrow. That is a misunderstanding of the inherent meaning of an eschatological faith. When Christian missionaries and theologians have acted narrowly and exclusivistically, they have implicitly betrayed the meaning of the Christian gospel for the history of religions. The Christian gospel does not set Christianity into the world as one among many other religions, which is to perpetuate its own identity through a contrast mentality that has characterized much of Christian history. But it is also a betrayal of the inclusivism, openness, and universalism that eschatological faith projects in relation to other religions.

Paul Tillich is right when he says, "The present attitude of Christianity to the world religions is as indefinite as that in most of its history."[5] This indefiniteness becomes conspicuous at many points, but we will consider three: methodological, dogmatic, and missiological. In our discussion we will be driving toward the establishment of our thesis that the theology and practice of mission should be projected within the horizon of an eschatological faith that links its own future in a promising way to the fulfilling future toward which all religions—by the fact that they are religions—are implicitly or explicitly striving.

## METHODOLOGICAL REFLECTIONS

At the beginning of our century a new school of theology arose that dealt with Christianity as one religion among the religions. It was given one of those roller-coasting German names, *Religionsgeschichtlicheschule*. It studied the history of religions with a view to comparisons and causal connections. Thus in English it is often called "The School of Comparative Religions." Ernst Troeltsch was its leading systematic theologian. Most other theological schools responded to this movement as an enemy that planned to cut out the heart of Christianity. The claim of Christianity to be unique and to be *the* religion with the only true revelation of the one living God in history was relativized. If Christianity swims in the river of history, it keeps its head above water in the same way all other religions do. And as a religion it has no more right to claim to have reached the shore, while still swimming, than the others.

The relativizing of the absolute claim of Christianity provoked a massive backlash in theology and stimulated the search for emergency measures to cope with the threat of historical relativism. The theology of Karl Barth is the backlash; the theology of Rudolf Bultmann the emergency measure. In saying this I am aware that others are free and more than willing to call what I propose "an emergency measure." And in one sense I accept that, for the Christian mission in world history, driven by eschatological faith, is itself an emergency measure. It arose as the reflex action of the "eschatological-already" in the midst of the "historical-not-yet"! In the words of New Testament scholarship it was the "postponement of the parousia" that sobered up the early Christians—intoxicated as they were on eschatological wine — so that they would go out into history on a mission of hope to all the world.

The Barthian backlash disengaged Christianity from the history of religions and relocated it in the history of revelation outside religion. Christianity as a religion can be compared to the other religions, but the results of this approach do not count for or against the claim that God has revealed himself solely in his Word, as mediated through Christ, the Bible, and the church. Segregation of theology from the study of the living world religions was the effect of this backlash. At best it could contrast divine revelation with human religion, with no aim at integration. The shattering attacks on religion in the modern period—by Feuerbach, Comte, Marx, and Freud —were all sustained by letting the religious side of Christianity shield and protect its revelatory side. In no way could the revelatory side be subjected to the criticism of historical reason. The Christian revelation and the history of religions stand pretty much outside each other —in a state of mutual exclusion and indifference.

In Rudolf Bultmann the detachment of the Christian revelation from the history of religions is carried out with remarkable consistency. The decision of faith today is an inner-existential act out of sight of the world's religions. And it occurs in response to a demythologized kerygma, that is, a message drained of the religious contents that hailed from Jewish apocalypticism and Hellenistic gnosticism. This means that faith and the kerygma are not only lifted out of the history of religions, but the religions of history are lifted out of them, reducing them to empty terms, to pure existential forms without historical contents. This is what I call an "emergency measure." Faith is free to make any claim it wishes about its unique kerygma because there is no way that religious historical studies could test or contest that claim and render it vulnerable.

Dietrich Bonhoeffer made another response to the relativization of Christianity's claim to be the absolute religion. He called for a nonreligious interpretation of biblical concepts. Christianity as a religion and all other religions have been surpassed by the secular age. If the Christian gospel is to live in today's world, it must be translated into secular terms, with no religious remainder. The left-wing followers of Bonhoeffer have taken this to mean a theology without God-language, since "God" is the most religious word of all. Along this line, the chief problem is no longer Christianity's relation to non-Christian religions, but instead the challenge of the modern secular world that has outgrown all religions as such and left them talking to themselves.

The Barth-Bultmann-Bonhoeffer line is a progressive withdrawal of Christianity from the scientific study of religions. Christian theology becomes autonomous, opting for home rule. On the other side, religious scholarship counters with its own move toward autonomy, so that psychology of religion, sociology of religion, history of religion, and phenomenology of religion become attached to objectifying methods that bracket out all theological interests or perspectives. Thus we are faced with an intolerable dualism. An eschatological faith with a historic mission that announces the future of the history of religions withdraws into a safe ghetto, where its own claims become invulnerable—and also irrelevant. Outside the ghetto the phenomenological method has the open field to itself; not wanting to be anybody's handmaid, it becomes a case of "art for art's sake" in the sphere of religion.

However useful the phenomenological method is proving to be in getting inside a religion and letting it speak for itself, it finally generates questions that cannot be answered within its own limits. It can only take a scholar so far, and is thus a preparatory method. It prepares the way for making a judgment about the particular religion in question, with respect to its claim to power, meaning, and truth. Such a judgment will involve the use of a criterion that cannot be separated from one's view of man—of what is truly human. If the scholar prescinds from this judgment, and therefore from any explicit criterion, he becomes a naïve phenomenologist who assumes that the structures of religious experience are fundamentally the same in all times and places, and that therefore if one looks hard enough, one can find parallel symbols and similar patterns expressing the same underlying phenomena. In this way the timeless ideas of Platonism become the operative presuppositions guiding the phenomenological analysis. And history has gone by the board. When one reads Mircea Eliade's phenomenological studies, one gets the impression of a pot-pourri of religious concepts and symbols that hail from the most diverse times and places, as though the particular historical situations in which they arose can be flicked away as so much external husk. The assumption is that the historical particularities are the transitory elements that have no fundamental meaning for the religious phenomena. This is not far from Fichte's dictum that "only the metaphysical, not the historical, saves." One has to ask whether the phenomenological method does not imply an ontology that is crypto-Platonic.

The phenomenological method has to be supplemented by a historical hermeneutic of religious phenomena that sees every religion in its givenness as the result of a historical process. Religions are not eternal but temporal; they come and they go; they are born and they change in the flux of history. What is true of the religion of Israel is also true of Christianity; only a moving picture can represent them in their contingent historical reality, and not a series of snapshots of their essential structures. This moving picture will not pay attention merely to a religion as it essentially is, but also to what it historically becomes. The actual history of any religion is always surpassing itself, entering into relationships with other religions, sometimes dying in the process, sometimes rising into new forms. Religions have an inherent drive to contact and overcome the others insofar as they claim to deal with the whole of reality. Interreligious conflict is due to the inner tendency of each religion to claim to be the true religion, as offering the true revelation or the true way of salvation. It is natural to religion to claim to answer the fundamental question of human existence. As Tillich says, that "is the question of the intrinsic aim of existence—in Greek, the *telos* of all existing things."[6] It is self-contradictory for a religion to allow for an ultimate *telos* besides the one it projects for itself. Religions, especially of the monotheistic type, have a tendency toward universality; they envisage one future for all things, because there is but one God who alone is the power determining all things from beginning to end.

The fact is, however, that we are faced in actual history with a plurality of religions. According to an ancient myth, there was originally only one religion, but after the fall, or at least since the Tower of Babel, many religions came into being on account of man's rebellion. The modern scientific study of religious origins gives us no reason to accept this myth. Nevertheless, this is no reason to reject the myth, only to interpret it differently. The idea—shall we say the hope— of one universal religion uniting all mankind points to the future, not to the past. The plurality of religions may be converging upon a common eschaton—the eschatological future that has the power to draw all things unto himself. The unity of the religions does not lie in a common anthropological structure that can be phenomenologically described. Rather, it is something that has yet to be worked out through the mission of the kingdom of God in history. All religions and the cultures they represent are opening into a universal history, so that the question of the ultimate unity of the religions can be meaningfully posed. The hope of the mission is that finally all fences and walls between the religions will be obliterated, and the vision of all men existing in unity and peace will be realized. When the eschatological empowerment of this hope has vanished, the hope itself is overpowered by the sight of the plurality of religions and hope becomes hopeless.

## DOGMATIC REFLECTIONS

The Christian mission is today reeling in a state of near hopelessness. It is not encouraged by what is going on in the world. Some predictions foresee that Christianity will become a minority religion in the not too distant future. Does not this make all talk about Christian eschatology as the projected future of the world religions quite outlandish? For this reason it is necessary to make clear what we are prepared to hold as Christian doctrine and what is only our personal speculation on the matter of the relation between Christianity and the non-Christian religions.

I would like to propose that as Christians we might agree on four dogmatic propositions, however we may work out their systematic connections and their speculative implications. First, Jesus Christ is the personal event in whom eschatological revelation has occurred, so that in history "we do not look for another" (Matt. 11:3). Second, faith in Jesus Christ means real personal participation in eschatological salvation. Third, the church is a community of believers who have the task to proclaim eschatological salvation to the whole world until the kingdom comes in its fullness. Fourth, it is God's will that all shall be saved and that the whole creation, now in a struggle for its life, will at last reach its fulfilling future through Christ himself.

The systematic problem is how to conceive the attainment of the universal goal by particular means. In the history of Christianity there has always been a fight between the particularists and the universalists. The particularists have classically stressed the concretely historical pole either in a more typically Catholic way or in a more Protestant way. The Catholic way avails itself of Cyprian's formula: outside the church there is no salvation. The Protestant way insists that salvation is only possible through personal faith in Jesus Christ. If we hold unqualifiedly to these concrete conditions of salvation, it is obvious that by far the majority of people in the world are doomed to be damned. The universal goal must appear unrealistic and the Christian mission must become something like salvaging human cargo from a ship that is headed for eternal disaster. Only a few make it into the ark of salvation; the rest perish in the flood. This view of things brings cheer to the particularists, but makes the universalists depressed. The particularists see that Christianity is radically exclusive; the universalists with equal zeal want to expand the definition of Christianity to make it radically inclusive. The fight continues to our day.

I am committed to the position that both sides are right in what they affirm and wrong in what they deny. The particularist affirms the basic Christian faith that salvation has really arrived in Jesus Christ and through his *ekklesia*. But as a rule the particularist denies the hope of universal salvation. Perhaps he adheres to a doctrine of double predestination, or single predestination, or free will and moral responsibility, such that he cannot postulate a real ultimate salvation for the *whole* world. He begins as a monist—the whole creation coming from One God, the Creator of all things; but he ends as a dualist—the whole creation eternally split in two, a small fraction getting to heaven, the rest going to hell.

The universalist wants all things to reach their intended destiny in the kingdom of freedom and fulfillment. The divine will to save all mankind will not miscarry. God does not believe in *apartheid,* so why should we project it into eternity? The split condition of humanity in history will ultimately be resolved into the unity of eternal life, when God will be all-in-all. This universal vision has been projected in two different ways. There is the humanistic universalism which denies the particularities of the Christian faith, on the grounds that everyone is too good to deserve to be damned; and there is a theocentric universalism, which affirms the particularities of faith but holds that the power of grace unto salvation will somehow win in the end, in spite of all present opposition.

There is a lot of room for speculation on how to understand this enigmatic "somehow." Early Christian apologetics used the idea of the Logos as the magic key by which non-Christians could enter the kingdom of heaven. In this way the apologists, who happened to be Christian philosophers, could hold out hope that their pagan colleagues could escape damnation. Socrates, Plato, and Aristotle were almost sure to make it, because they carried a good measure of the universal Logos within them. Quite inconsistently, many particularists who insisted on salvation only through conscious belief in Christ still made room for the noble pagans. I say this is "inconsistent" because, in doing so, they are meeting the universalists at least halfway. They are acknowledging that in principle salvation *is* possible apart from explicit faith in Jesus Christ. They are saying that noble pagans can be saved through intellectual and moral enlightenment, a concept that must be shattered by their own doctrine of original sin and *sola gratia*.

Karl Rahner is a present-day exponent of a way of salvation to the noble pagans, only he calls them "anonymous Christians."[7] The unbelievers have moved up one notch in Christian vocabulary. The problem with the idea of "noble pagans" and "anonymous Christians" is that it betrays a Christian elitism that does not befit a religion of radical grace. Only the elite in every religion can ever make it, all those people that papal encyclicals refer to "as men of good will." But then who picks up the rotten apples, the bad guys, the hopelessly lost, the real sinners? The test of an adequate universalism is not a Socrates, because all admit heaven would be unimaginably boring without him; rather, the acid test is a Hitler, an Eichmann, and other degenerate pimps of the system that crucify the Jew of Galilee and all his "little ones" in the world.

If Christians make room for only the good people in heaven, this is the wrong way to speculate on whether non-Christians can "somehow or other" attain unto salvation. There's not much hope that can be derived from putting trust in the goodness of people. A much better way is that of Karl Barth, whose universalism is grounded exclusively in the goodness of grace—God's election of all mankind in Jesus Christ.[8] Jesus Christ is the double predestination, with the rejection and the election of all men occurring in him. Jesus Christ is the only person who is realy rejected, the only reprobate man. Apart from Jesus Christ there is none who is rejected on his own. The rejection of men has been taken up into the rejection of Jesus Christ, so that they can participate fully also in his election. There is a universalism of grace, not of merit. In an ultimate sense there is none who is lost; there is no eternal condemnation, no everlasting hell, no final judgment that is not overtaken by the superior decision of grace.

Barth's doctrine is attractive; it achieves its universalism through a high doctrine of the centrality of Christ. However, he loses us when he backs the election of Christ for all men into a prehistory, into the eternal pre-existence of the God-Man. He seems to tear the process of redemption out of the sphere of history, and plants it in a time before all time. We cannot deal more extensively with Barth's doctrine of election,[9] except to state that its a-historical character is largely due to a defective eschatology—an eschatology that proved to be allergic to history. This type of eschatology can hardly motivate the Christian mission within the horizon of the world's religions.

The tension between the historical particularity of Christianity and its eschatological universalism is capable of a different type of speculative resolution. The kingdom of God which Jesus proclaimed and which he pioneered in his own ministry of life, death, and resurrection can be seen retrospectively to be the power at work in all the religions of mankind. The God who is coming with his kingdom, with his power and glory, is present to all epochs prior to Christ and outside the Christian sphere as the power of their end. The eschatological light of God's coming kingdom that shines in Christ flashes back upon all the religions as the end to which they are pointing. Retroactively they are all claimed and converted into witnesses to the coming of the fullness of truth beyond their own limitations. The eschaton that becomes really present in Jesus is the dynamic of the apostolic mission whose essential purpose is to announce the comprehensive universality of that eschaton for all people yesterday, today, and forevermore. The eschatological validity of God's saving power in Jesus' history could not be maintained as the subject matter of the universal mission if he did not mediate the comprehensive future of all the world's religions. For then some other future apart from the future of God in Christ would be their goal, and thus their Lord.

Thus, the universal pole is reinforced by the concrete historical pole of the Christian faith. For to the extent that we take the history of Jesus and his meaning to the early Christians seriously in their terms, to that extent we will enter into a thoroughly penetrating eschatological consciousness that came to express itself through the universal mission of apostolic Christianity. That is, the particularity of Jesus and his gospel enkindles the universal flame that spreads throughout the world, bringing the light of truth and the warmth of love.

## MISSIOLOGICAL REFLECTIONS

The eschatological future of the world which Jesus represented is now verifying its universal validity through the mission to the world. The world is incomplete; its future is still unknown; what it will become in the end is anybody's theory. Those who preach the gospel are making a sort of wager while the race is still on: *the truth in Jesus bears the final revelation of the future of the world.* The truth of the world and of its religions is not manifest in what they already are in themselves, in their incompleteness; it is only manifest through the promise of what they are at last to become. Christ is the manifestation of the truth of what all things shall become in their fullness, the power of what things essentially are in their final future.

This eschatological orientation of the universal mission has innumerable practical implications, of which we will indicate only three: first, the primary task of the mission is the proclamation of the gospel of the kingdom of God. Of utmost importance in this gospel is the element of the comprehensive universality of the kingdom as the salvation for the whole world. Second, the mission operates within the horizon of the challenge that the world has not yet been penetrated with the knowledge of its own future in the kingdom of God. The universality of the truth that has arrived in Jesus of Nazareth and is now advanced by the mission is an eschatological reality that exists beyond the frontiers of the church. The church is not yet universal; its catholicity is an attribute of the kingdom, and therefore of the church only insofar as it already is a participation of the eschatological kingdom. Practically this means that the church humbly shows to the other religions that it is also on the way, and is not the goal itself. This will help to break down the resistance that every finite movement generates in others when it claims to be the final thing. Only eschatological consciousness in the church can relativize its own haughty triumphalism, and all its arrogant talk about having an absolute authority, an inerrant book, or an infallible office. The church is always weakest when it claims too much. An overstatement of the claim alienates others who should be allowed to participate in universal salvation without being put off by a scandalous church. Third, the present mission to the world, whether in its secular or its religious manifestations, has not yet been articulated in an adequate way by such old-fashioned terms as "converting the heathen" or "planting the church," nor by such new-fashioned terms as "inter-religious dialogue" or "Christian presence." A more adequate way will emerge when the eschatological dimensions of the mission are more fully recovered. Then the radically inclusive power of the gospel will send the mission into the stream of world history to embrace its pluralities within a universalism of hope.

The petering-out of eschatology as the driving power of the mission will always produce ersatz proposals about the church's mission to the world. Some of these are hopeless *tours de force*, tactics of desperation. It is as though Christianity is feeling old in its bones; its era is passing with the decline of the West. A few survivors set themselves *à la recherche du temps perdu*, with Marcel Proust. But romanticism is not the Christian way of recovering youth or of escaping a dragging present. Only the eschatological way, a rebirth of the symbols of the apocalypse of Jesus, can make Christianity again very new and very young, always out in front of the passing parade of new religions succeeding old ones in the struggle for a future that can bind them to a permanent fulfillment. The religion of the future will be the one that can best project the most fulfilling future of religion.

### NOTES

1. Paul Tillich, "The Significance of the History of Religions for the Systematic Theologian," *The Future of Religions* (New York: Harper & Row, 1966), p. 91.

2. *Ibid.*

3. Karl Rahner, "Christianity and the Non-Christian Religions," *Theological Investigations,* Vol. V (Baltimore: Helicon Press, 1966), p. 116.

4. Paul Tillich, *Christianity and the Encounter of the World Religions* (New York: Columbia University Press, 1963), p. 82.

5. *Ibid.,* p. 46.

6. *Ibid.,* p. 63.

7. Karl Rahner, *op. cit.,* pp. 133ff.

8. Karl Barth, *Church Dogmatics,* trans. by G. W. Bromiley *et al.* (Edinburgh: T. & T. Clark, 1957), II/2, pp. 94ff.

9. The best study of Barth's doctrine of election is by Robert W. Jenson, *Alpha and Omega* (New York: Thomas Nelson, 1963).

# Index

# Index of Names